DELICIOUS GIFTS

Creations to Make and Give

DELICIOUS GIFTS

Tasty Creations to Make and Give

JESS McCLOSKEY

Search Press

This edition published in 2011 by
Search Press Ltd
Wellwood
North Farm Road
Tunbridge Wells
Kent TN2 3DR
www.searchpress.com

A Quintet book

This book was conceived, designed and produced by
Quintet Publishing Limited, The Old Brewery, 6 Blundell Street,
London N7 9BH, UK

Project Editor: Martha Burley
Consultant and Copyeditor: Cary Hull
Designers: Bonnie Bryan and Zoë White
Illustrator: Jane Laurie
Photographer: Ian Garlick
Home Economist: Marie-Ange Lapierre
Props Stylist: Zoë White
Art Director: Michael Charles
Managing Editor: Donna Gregory
Publisher: Mark Searle

Printed by 1010 Printing International Ltd, China

ISBN: 978-1-8444-8749-3

10 9 8 7 6 5 4 3 2 1

CONTENTS

Introduction

Homemade presents are a joy to receive. They can be touchingly personal and endearingly messy, but they also come with the knowledge that someone spent time and effort to make them. When you receive a homemade gift, you can't help but feel special.

The person who makes and gives a homemade present feels special too – it is just so incredibly rewarding to create a gift with your own hands. There is a wonderful simplicity in making an old jar beautiful with a piece of ribbon or in crafting a box out of colourful card, and then filling it with something delicious made in your own kitchen. It takes us back to a simpler time of in-person conversations, quality items made with care and genuine acts of love.

Of course, it is faster and arguably 'easier' to buy a gift card or order a gift online, but there is no comparison to the joy that comes from making and giving – or in receiving – a beautiful handmade gift.

Some of the best gifts from the kitchen come cobbled together from what you have to hand, not from some expensive and hard-to-find ingredients. For instance, my recipes don't require that you use the best quality of chocolate. If you want to save money by using a lower quality, give it a try – all chocolate has charm!

My recipes for delicious gifts don't need a great deal of practice or any particular culinary skills. There are only a couple of slightly more complex recipes sprinkled throughout (I won't name them, for fear of putting you off a delicious treat), and even those are easily dealt with by following the directions carefully. You should not worry about being 'perfect' – the joy of making and receiving a homemade gift is that it is different from what you can buy in shops.

It's very easy to adapt these recipes to individual tastes or what you have to hand. Feel free to change any ingredients that you want. Substitute one chocolate for another, throw in extra nuts, experiment with different flavourings, try something new – use these recipes as a launch pad and make something really wonderful for your loved ones.

Creating delicious food should be fun and as devoid of pressure as possible. So dive in, try something out and show someone how great they (and you!) are.

KITCHEN UTENSILS AND EQUIPMENT

You do not need every kitchen gadget available to create the delicious gifts in this book.
Check to see what you've already got in your kitchen. Here are some of my favourites.

SUGAR THERMOMETER

While you can drop cooked confectionary into cold water to determine its stage, a sugar thermometer takes away all the guesswork. Make sure it has a protected base (so that the gauge never touches the bottom of the pan) and never store it in your junk drawer – they can be fragile.

BAKING TRAYS

It takes a bit of experimentation to determine if you prefer glass, silicone or metal baking pans. Start with a basic 23x32-cm (9x13-in) baking tin and a muffin tin and work up from there.

DIPPING FORKS AND TOOLS

These sets are absolute sanity-savers when you are dipping in melted chocolate. Most sets come with at least a fork and a little metal circle on a stick; there are fancier sets if you really get into the world of chocolate.

CHOCOLATE MOULDS

Making homemade chocolates is a whole lot easier and more satisfying once you start using chocolate moulds, because the results are so unfailingly beautiful. You can even find moulds that let you make filled truffles.

BISCUIT CUTTERS

Use them on biscuits, yes, but cutters can also be used to cut marshmallows, fudges and cakes. Anything that will hold its shape can be cut.

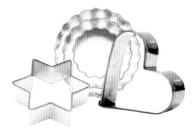

ELECTRIC WHISK OR FOOD PROCESSOR

Everything in this book can be mixed by hand, but an electric whisk or food processor can make a faster job of it. A simple hand-held whisk is my everyday tool of choice.

PESTLE AND MORTAR

Most chopping can be done on a cutting board with a big knife, but when I need something crushed, nothing works better than an old-fashioned pestle and mortar. Choose one that has a solid base and feels good in your hand.

PIPING BAG AND TIPS

It is tempting to run out and buy a fancy set of bags and tips as soon as you see what they can do. With a small beginners' kit, however, you can easily create professional, beautiful designs on your confections. You could also use a heavy plastic bag with a corner cut off (see how to drizzle on page 12).

NON-STICK BAKING SHEET

These baking sheets (which are often made of silicone) are absolutely invaluable in the kitchen. They are roll-able, cut-able, reusable sheets that can be used to line pans or used as a resting spot for confections to set.

WHISKS AND SPATULAS

There are some jobs where a spoon simply doesn't work – these are the times when you need to have a whisk or a spatula on hand. Whisks allow you to really sieve together dry ingredients and spatulas help you get every last bit of a batter out of the bowl.

ROLLING PIN

While it is possible to do without, a rolling pin is incredibly useful for several kitchen tasks. All you really need is a solid weighted pin that feels good in your hands. Marble is wonderful because it stays cool, while wood is very easy to use.

EDIBLE DECORATIONS

The recipe has been tried and tested, it tastes divine, and you're ready to package your gift. Before you wrap it up, there is a world of different decorative methods at your disposal to give your gift that truly unique touch.

CANDY COATINGS

If you have a lot of items to cover or if you find coating in chocolate difficult to get right (cake bites can be a little bit tricky if you're not used to working with soft, potentially crumbly balls), then using a candy coating (also called confectioners' coating) can be a real lifesaver. These are made to be particularly easy to melt (they contain various shortenings so they melt easily and retain a shine after they set) and use. You can get them in a wide range of

flavours and colours, so you can experiment with what you like. I especially like the white chocolate candy coating, but beware of using them for particularly rich chocolate desserts, as chocolate lovers can taste the difference.

CHOCOLATE COATING

To use chocolate as a coating, you need to melt it first. There are three main ways to do this. While there is a lot of discussion about which is the best method, it really comes down to doing what is easiest. Try them all to discover which is most foolproof for you.

Double Boiler: You can easily improvise a double boiler. The chocolate rests in a bowl or pan that sits on top of boiling water. In this way, the chocolate is never in direct contact with the heat source and therefore avoids the dangers of scorching.

Direct Heat: Simply melt the chocolate in a pan on the stove. This is a great method because it is quick and easy, but it is one of the more dangerous methods because it is all too easy to scorch the chocolate. So always use a low heat and stir throughout. This method works best when you are using the chocolate as an ingredient and don't necessarily need it to be well-tempered.

Microwave Oven: Using the microwave is my preferred method as it allows me to temper the chocolate, yet isn't as complex as using a double boiler. Heat in short bursts (30 seconds is ideal), stirring each time you stop. Remove the chocolate from the microwave before it is fully melted. The heat from the melted chocolate will continue to warm up the remaining chunks so that they can be stirred down after a few minutes.

Once you have successfully melted your chocolate, it is ready to be used as a covering for your sweets and treats. If you want to half cover an item – such as a large pretzel or biscuit – simply dip it into the chocolate and drag it across the rim of the bowl to remove any excess. Place on a non-stick sheet or baking tray while the chocolate dries.

If you want to fully cover a confection, a dipping fork and other tools can be invaluable. Drop the confection into the chocolate and turn it gently, using your tool, until it is fully covered. Remove from the chocolate and place it on your sheet or tray. Once it has set, you can repeat the entire process of dipping to give you a full, smooth coverage that has no 'feet' – the little rings of chocolate that can sometimes occur when the melting chocolate pools at the base of the confection. If you like those bits of chocolate, though, don't worry about a second coating – handmade should be a little bit rustic looking!

You can also just put a drizzle of chocolate on the top of a sweet or confection, which can be charming and give it a finishing touch. Luckily, it's also quite easy to accomplish. If you are happy with a more casual look, you can simply dip a fork into melted chocolate (you may want to let the first big dollop drip back into the bowl to prevent having a huge drop where you weren't expecting it) and then wave it back and forth over your sweet. You'll be left with lovely little streaks of chocolate.

If you want a more precise look, simply fill a heavy plastic bag with the chocolate and cut off the tip of the bag to create a makeshift piping bag (a small snip results in thinner streaks, while larger holes give you much wider ones); you can, of course, also use a shop-bought piping bag.

EDIBLE GLITTER

Edible glitter and pearlescent shimmer are rightfully very popular – they are attractive and very easy to use. There are several kinds of glitter available, from those that melt when they get wet to tiny cut-out shapes, so there is plenty to explore.

FOOD COLOURING

There are several types of food colouring, including gels, powders and liquids. What kind you use is wholly dependent upon what you want to colour. When working with chocolate, it is important to only use gels or powder, because liquid food colouring will cause the chocolate to seize.

TIP

White chocolate is by far the easiest to work with, with milk chocolate not far behind. Dark chocolate can be a bit trickier, so make sure that you practise on the easier chocolates first.

CHOCOLATE CURLS

Chocolate curls look like they take skill, talent and more time than the average person has to spare. As they are actually incredibly easy to make, this makes them perfect for impressing your recipient with a professional-looking decoration on your homemade gift.

You will need a good, sharp vegetable peeler that is perfectly dry. Have a dry bowl or plate ready for your shavings as you make them, plus a wooden skewer to easily move them around. Allow your chocolate to warm to a toasty room temperature. This can be done on top of your refrigerator or near a warm oven, but avoid using actual heating methods such as the microwave or stove – you want room temperature and no more, otherwise you can accidentally melt your chocolate.

1 Cover your work surface with parchment paper or aluminium foil, bringing it near the edge of the counter.

2 Place your chocolate bar on the edge of the counter, with any scoring or embellishments facing down (you want the smooth surface facing you as you work). You need to put light pressure on the chocolate bar, so it is good to cover the chocolate with a bit of parchment paper where your hand is touching. This prevents you from melting the chocolate with the warmth of your hand.

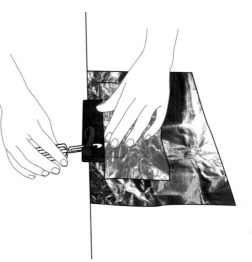

3 Draw the peeler down the narrow edge of the chocolate in a smooth stroke, bringing the curl of chocolate with you so that it does not break. Gently transfer the curls to your bowl or plate to rest until you are ready to use them.

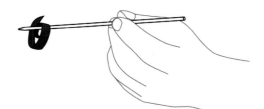

4 You can use the curls immediately or place them in the refrigerator, covered, until needed. They will keep just fine for at least a week.

TIP
Always ensure that your tools and containers are completely dry when working with chocolate.

RECYCLING AND DECORATING JARS

When you want to make preserves or give a gift in a glass container, there is no reason to run out and buy a new jar. Look around your kitchen and you'll find a whole host of usable containers.

STERILISING JARS

If you want to make a preserved food item that will stay safe to eat for a length of time, it is important to sterilise the jar before filling. For a glass jar to be completely free from any contaminants, it must be exposed to relatively high levels of heat for a sustained period of time. Always start with clean, well-scrubbed jars.

A quick and easy method is to simply run the jars and lids through a long cycle (with steam cleaning and hot drying) in a dishwasher right before you fill them. Jars (but not their metal lids) can also be heated in a microwave oven. Fill the jar halfway with water and place in the microwave on high for 2–3 minutes, until the water boils. Remove, discard the water and use immediately.

Traditional sterilising methods are boiling on the hob or oven heating. For boiling, place the jars in a large straight-sided saucepan without their lids; the jars can touch, but do not overlap them (see 1, right).

Fill the straight-sided saucepan with water until the jars are completely submerged. Bring to the boil and then boil for 10 minutes before removing and filling (see 2, right). If using a dry ingredient, be sure there is no remaining moisture in the jar.

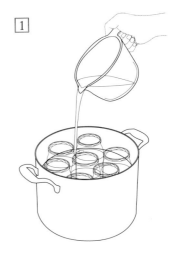

TIP
Sticky label refusing to budge? Try rubbing pure dish detergent on the label and letting it sit for a couple of hours before soaking it in hot soapy water. For seriously sticky labels, a bit of vinegar will do the trick.

OVEN-STERILISING JARS

For oven heating, make sure your jars are clean and well-scrubbed (see 1, below). Place jars on a sheet pan and heat in a 100°C (200°F) oven for 10–12 minutes (see 2, below). Remove and fill.

1

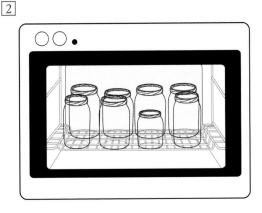

2

STERILISING LIDS

To sterilise the lids, submerge them in water in a saucepan (they should not overlap) and bring to the boil. Let boil for 10 minutes before using.

DECORATING WITH RIBBONS

The effect of a lovely ribbon on a present cannot be overstated, but it is worth thinking about finding a bit of decoration where you don't expect it. Raffia, yarn and bits of spare cloth and leather all make for wonderfully unique ribbons that can dress up a gift jar.

MAKING LABELS

A handmade label will not only identify who the recipient and giver are, but it can be a decorative element in its own right. Many found items can be constructed into something special: try making labels out of cloth, parchment paper, foil or even beautiful autumn leaves.

MAKING AND COVERING GIFT BOXES

When you have put in the time and effort to create your delicious treats, you want the presentation to be just as striking as the tasty treat inside.

HANDCRAFTED BOXES

Making your own boxes is surprisingly easy and can actually be quite an enjoyable way to use up some spare paper and ribbon.

Handcrafted boxes can be made in two ways – the first is to make the box entirely from scratch, and the second is to cover an existing box with attractive paper.

If you are making the box from scratch, a standard card is sufficient for holding truffles or other light confections. If you want a sturdier box, use a heavier weight. Use a basic white glue or a craft glue; a glue gun can also be used.

When covering a box, lighter papers work better. Any craft or tissue paper will work; use a lighter glue to avoid lumps.

MAKING A SIMPLE HINGED RECTANGULAR BOX

This box is perfect for small treats such as the Brown Sugar and Butter Magic Brittle on page 71.

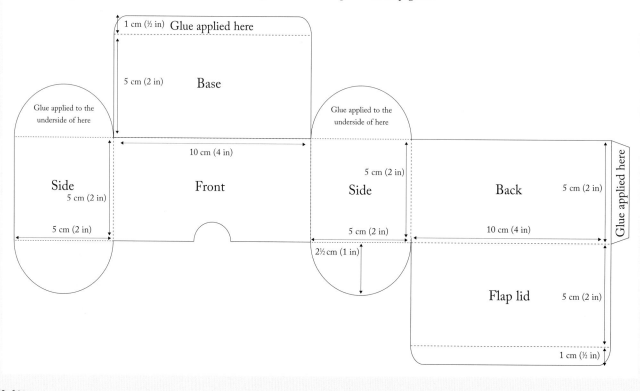

1 Trace around the template on the cardstock you have chosen for the box. Cut it out with sharp scissors or use a straight edge and a knife and fold along all edges.

2 Apply glue to the rounded tabs indicated on the net and fold round to fix them to the base.

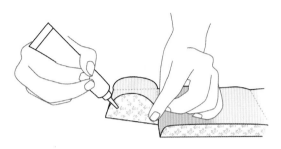

3 Glue along the long tab on the base of the box.

4 Glue along the short tab and bring the back of the box up, slotting the side tab in to complete the box.

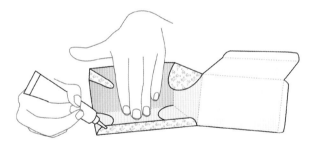

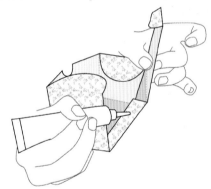

TIP

The simple hinged rectangular box is an absolute classic and suits just about every kind of confection. Choose a sturdy coloured card so there is no need to cover it.

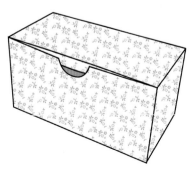

MAKING A SIMPLE RECTANGULAR BOX WITH LID

A classic favourite, the lidded box could be used to present a gift like the Dark Chocolate and Marmalade Bars on page 40.

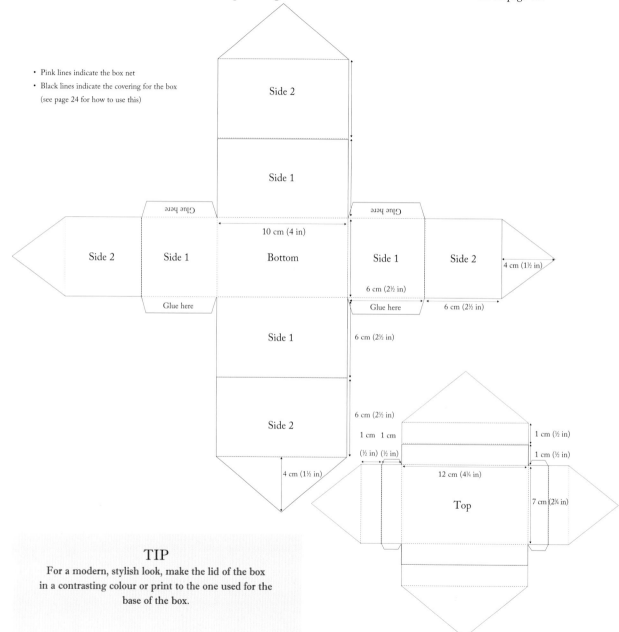

- Pink lines indicate the box net
- Black lines indicate the covering for the box
  (see page 24 for how to use this)

Side 2

Side 1

Glue here

Side 2   Side 1   Bottom   Side 1   Side 2   4 cm (1½ in)

Glue here

10 cm (4 in)

6 cm (2½ in)

Glue here   Glue here   6 cm (2½ in)

Side 1   6 cm (2½ in)

6 cm (2½ in)

1 cm 1 cm   1 cm (½ in)

(½ in) (½ in)   1 cm (½ in)

Side 2   12 cm (4¼ in)

7 cm (2¾ in)

4 cm (1½ in)   Top

TIP

For a modern, stylish look, make the lid of the box
in a contrasting colour or print to the one used for the
base of the box.

1 Trace around the template on your chosen card. Cut along the outline with sharp scissors or use a straight edge and a knife. Fold in all the glue tabs toward the centre of the box, using a ruler or other straight edge to ensure you get a very straight line.

2 Working from the narrow end of the box, apply glue to the glue tabs and match them to the edges on the longer side of the box.

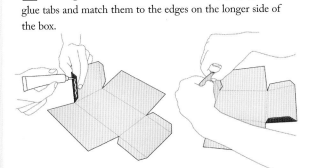

3 Allow to dry fully before filling the box.

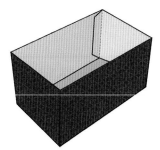

For the lid

4 Trace the template for the lid onto your card, cut it out and glue along the glue tab.

5 Be sure that the glue on the lid is fully dry before you put it on the box.

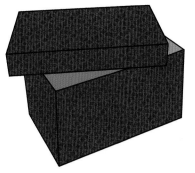

MAKING A ROUND BOX WITH LID

This versatile box could be used to wrap up pieces of scrumptious Mint and Chocolate Fudge (page 79) or Fruitcake and White Chocolate Truffles (page 38).

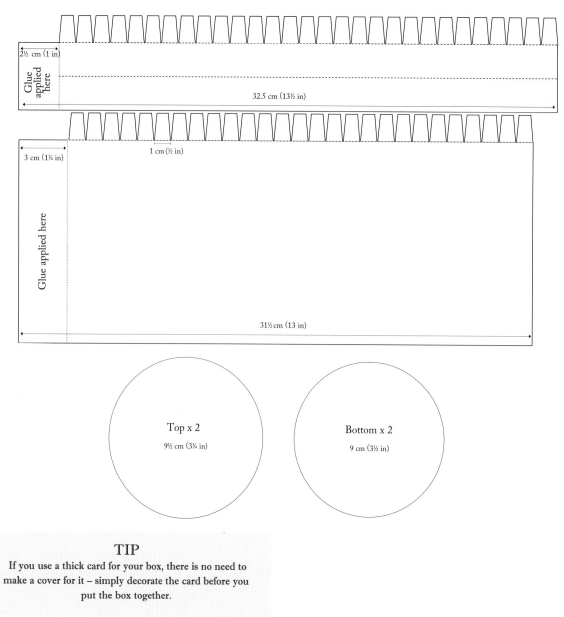

TIP

If you use a thick card for your box, there is no need to make a cover for it – simply decorate the card before you put the box together.

[1] Either follow the template or choose what the diameter of your container will be. Trace around a can or use a compass to draw a circle in your selected size on your card; this will be the bottom of your container. Cut it out with sharp scissors. Cut out a second circle (to cover the raw edges).

[2] Cut out a rectangle for the body of the box. Its length should be the circumference of the circle (remember that you can find the circumference of the circle by the diameter multiplied by 3.14), plus an additional 3 cm (1¼ in) for overlapping and gluing. The width of the rectangle will become the height of the box, with an added 1 cm (½ in) for gluing.

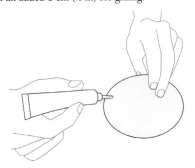

[3] Score a line along the length of the rectangle, where the 1-cm (½-in) glue line will be. Cut the card in short snips all along this length, to provide you with a cut glue line.

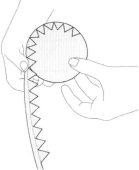

[4] Bend the snips in toward the centre of the circle. Apply glue to the edge of your first circle. Press the snipped end of the rectangle along the edge of the circle, forming a round box. Apply glue along the narrow edge of the rectangle and press down to fully form the box; clip together with a clothes peg until the glue dries.

[5] When the glue has dried, glue the second circle on top of the rough edges of the snipped edge to create a smooth finish.

Making the lid

Following the directions in Step 1 above, cut out two more circles for the top of the lid, but make them just slightly larger than you did for the bottom. This is so the lid can slide on and off the box.

Use the same length for the lid's rectangle as for the sides of the box, but remember when determining its width that you only need a lip of 2½ cm (1¼ in) or so for the lid.

MAKING A HEXAGONAL HINGED BOX

Don't let the ornate design fool you – this lovely little box is easy to make and great for stuffing with a couple of decadent truffles.

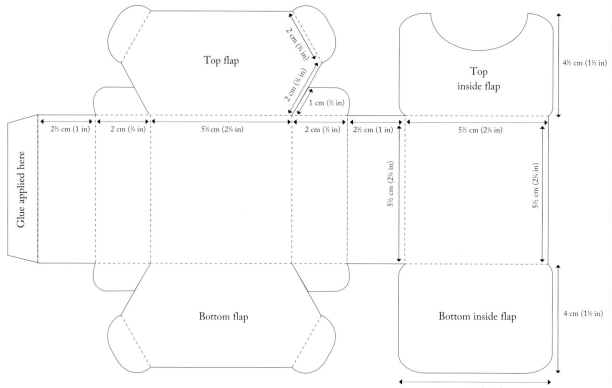

1 Trace around the template on the card that will become the box. Using a straight edge and knife or sharp scissors, cut out the box along the traced outline.

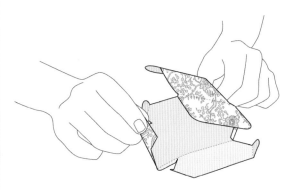

2 Using a ruler or straight edge to give a very straight line to work from, bend the glue tabs inwards, towards the inside of the box.

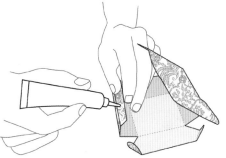

TIP
Hexagonal boxes are fetchingly unique; these quirky shapes best suit dramatic prints and the most outlandish of your paper designs.

3 Working from the longer side, fold the end back toward the other edge and glue the tab to the main portion of the card. Pinch the tabs together until the glue dries enough to hold the shape of the box.

4 Fold through the base of the box, gluing the tabs together as you work.

5 Fold over the top to close the box, without gluing.

COVERING A RECTANGULAR BOX

Whether you want to cover your own handmade box from page 18 with pretty paper or wish to reuse an old box, this method is faultless.

1 Trace the template shape form page 18 onto your decorative paper. Using a knife and straight edge or a pair of scissors, cut out the shape.

3 Place the box in the centre of the paper and bring the sides of the paper up over the sides of the box. Fold the paper at the edges and glue it to the inside of the box.

5 When folding the paper over, pull the paper taut and fold along the edge precisely.

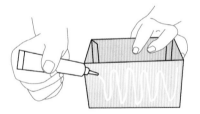

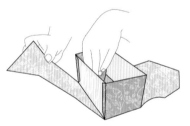

2 Apply glue to the sides of your box, inside and out.

4 Work your way around the entire box, tucking the edges of the covering paper into the interior of the box, smoothing the paper as you work.

6 If desired, cut out a rectangle of the decorative paper to glue into the bottom of the box.

TIP

Thin paper can be incredibly easy to work with and it's often where you'll find some of the most beautiful prints and colours. Unfortunately, if it is too thin, the glue beneath can show through and cause lumps in the covering. If you want to use a very thin paper, try using a glue stick instead of white glue for a smooth finish.

Covering the lid

Cover the lid in the same fashion.

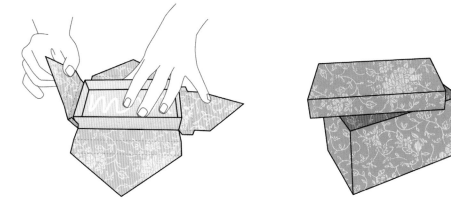

COVERING A ROUND BOX

To reinforce a weak box or cover unsightly card, follow the directions below (continues over the page).

1 Cut out the rectangle from the template, making small cuts along the long edge of paper to create the glue tabs. Ensure that the cuts go in no deeper than 1 cm (½ in). Trace and cut out the circle for the bottom of the box.

2 Apply glue to the outside of the circular box.

3 Wrap the decorative paper around the circular box, smoothing it as you work. Once the paper has been attached to the sides of the box, fold down the bottom tabs to form the bottom.

COVERING A ROUND BOX CONTINUED...

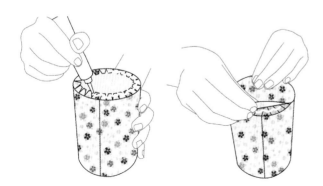

4 Applying more glue, attach the bottom circle. Working with the lid, trace and cut out all pieces for the covering.

6 Repeating the process, apply glue and attach the last strip to the inner ring of the lid.

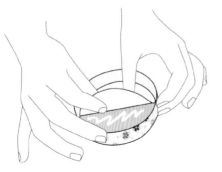

5 Applying glue to the outside of the lid, attach the thin rectangle to the edges of the lid and one circle to the outside. Apply glue and attach the final circle to the inside of the lid.

TIP
If you have only an ugly piece of card to work with, cover it with decorative paper.

MAKING A PARTITION FOR A BOX

Follow the instructions for making the simple hinged rectangular box (page 16). Allow the box to dry completely before making and inserting the partition.

1 Cut out two pieces of firm card for the partition. For the box on page 16, the partition will need to be 5 cm x 7.5 cm in size. Fold in two tabs at 1.25 cm from each end of the length. Fold both partition sheets at the ends, forming an "I" shape.

2 Glue together the center sections of the partition sheets.

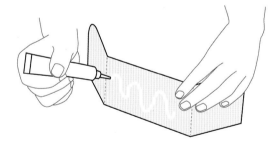

3 Hold the pieces together firmly until the glue has dried.

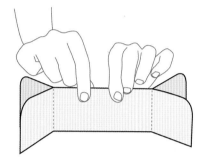

4 Insert the partition into the box and position it in the centre.

TIP
Using a large partitioned box not only allows for giving more confections without using more boxes, but it also makes for a dramatic, abundant-looking gift. Try putting together two items with contrasting colours for the most impact. For instance, pairing the White Chocolate and Blueberry Fudge with the Mint and Chocolate Fudge is absolutely gorgeous.

5 Fold back each of the edge pieces in turn, adding glue and pressing gently against the sides of the box. Wait until the glue is dry before filling the box with confections.

CHAPTER ONE

Truffles and Chocolates

Rich, luxurious and indulgent, who wouldn't love to receive a present of handmade truffles or chocolates? One of the most classic of treats, a truffle is surprisingly easy to make and can be adapted in many ways to personalise your gift.

WHITE CHOCOLATE TRUFFLES

Even if you don't normally choose white chocolate, that will be changed by these creamy, absolutely tempting delights. With the same smooth vanilla perfection of a high-quality white chocolate, yet with a softness that gives them richness, these truffles are melt-in-the-mouth delicious. Try adding different flavour – it is just about impossible to be anything but charmed by the addition of Baileys Irish Cream or coffee essence.

1 Place the white chocolate pieces in a heatproof glass bowl.

2 Add the butter and cream to a saucepan set over medium heat. Remove from heat as soon as the cream mixture just begins to bubble. Stir in the vanilla essence (or other flavouring).

3 Pour the cream mixture over the white chocolate pieces and allow to sit for a couple of minutes to let the heat of the mixture work its way through the chocolate. Stir gently until the chocolate melts and is incorporated into the mixture, forming a ganache.

4 Place the ganache in the refrigerator for at least 4 hours to set. If tightly covered, the ganache will keep well in the refrigerator for up to 2 weeks.

5 Using a teaspoon or tablespoon, scoop out a small amount of the ganache, depending on the size truffle you prefer. Shape with your hands into a smooth ball (anywhere from marble size to golfball size), and then place in a dish of icing sugar (or other coating). Roll back and forth until the truffles have been completely dusted.

6 Pack truffles into your gift container. Store in an airtight container in the refrigerator for up to 2 weeks.

TIP
If you want to increase the size of the batch, always ensure that you are keeping the same ratio of ingredients. If the truffle mix doesn't 'set', increase the amount of melted white chocolate.

MAKES 12–24

250 g (9 oz) broken white chocolate or white chocolate chips

80 g (3 oz) butter

80 ml (3 fl oz) thick cream

1 tsp vanilla essence (or substitute coffee, mint, cinnamon or orange essence or Baileys Irish Cream)

Icing sugar, for dredging (or substitute coconut, crushed nuts or dark unsweetened cocoa powder)

DARK CHOCOLATE TRUFFLES

Dark chocolate truffles are a classic for a reason – they are consistently one of the most delicious ways to get a chocolate lover to smile. With a few simple changes it's possible to make a highly personalised creation that will let your recipient know how much you care. With the addition of flavours to the ganache or by changing what the finished truffle is rolled in, each truffle can become its own little masterpiece.

MAKES 12–24

300 g (10½ oz) chopped dark chocolate (or use chocolate chips)

2 tbsp butter

180 ml (6 fl oz) thick cream

1 tbsp (or to taste) coffee essence, cognac or other flavouring (optional)

Dark unsweetened cocoa powder, for dredging (or substitute with crushed nuts, coconut or chocolate sprinkles)

1. Place the chocolate pieces in a heatproof glass bowl.

2. Add the butter and cream to a saucepan and gently bring to the boil. Remove from heat as soon as the mixture begins to bubble. Stir in flavouring, if using.

3. Pour the cream mixture over the chocolate and allow to sit for a couple of minutes to let the heat of the mixture work its way through the chocolate. Stir gently until the chocolate melts and is incorporated into the mixture, forming a ganache.

4. Place the ganache in the refrigerator for at least 4 hours to set. If tightly covered, the ganache will keep well in the refrigerator for up to 2 weeks.

5. Using a teaspoon or tablespoon, scoop out a small amount of the ganache, depending on the size of truffle you prefer. Shape with your hands into a smooth ball (anywhere from marble size to golfball size), and then place in a dish of dark unsweetened cocoa. Roll back and forth until the truffles have been completely dusted. Store in an airtight container in the refrigerator for up to 2 weeks.

TIP

Dark chocolate is a far more forgiving ganache than white chocolate and can easily be increased in size if you want a larger batch. By increasing the amount of cream, you can make a softer ganache, which is lovely when poured over a cake as an icing.

MILK CHOCOLATE COVERED PEANUT BUTTER MELTAWAYS

It's hard to beat the classic combination of chocolate and peanut butter. The slight saltiness of the peanut butter perfectly offsets the sweet creaminess of the chocolate. This version makes a light and fluffy peanut butter ganache, which elevates the traditional peanut butter cup into something recipients will remember long after they have finished off the last delicious piece.

1 Place peanut butter, softened butter and vanilla into a bowl. Stir briskly until all the ingredients are incorporated.

2 Stir in the icing sugar 1 cup at a time. Depending on the consistency of the peanut butter, the humidity in your kitchen, and your own personal tastes, it is possible to reduce the amount of sugar, so adding it slowly, stirring to form a stiff dough, is recommended. The dough should not be crumbly, but it will be stiff and dry to the touch. You should be able to hold it in your hands without it sticking to your skin.

3 Allow the peanut butter ganache to cool in the refrigerator until it fully stiffens – usually about 4 hours or, if desired, overnight. Then, use a teaspoon to scoop out dough and roll into balls of desired size.

4 Dip balls partially in the melted chocolate to make buckeye-style sweets or cover completely in chocolate to make truffles.

5 Allow to cool until the chocolate has firmed. This step can be sped up in the refrigerator. If desired, drizzle with melted white or dark chocolate. When firm, pack into gift boxes. Store in an airtight container in a cool location for up to 2 weeks.

TIP
If you work so slowly that the ganache begins to warm to room temperature and become sticky, simply re-chill the ganache and melt the chocolate just before rolling.

MAKES 24–48

400 g (14 oz) smooth peanut butter

225 g (8 oz) butter, softened

1 tsp vanilla essence

375 g (13 oz) icing sugar

250 g (9 oz) melted milk chocolate, dark chocolate or white chocolate to cover (or less if you aren't covering the entire batch), or use candy coating if preferred

STORAGE
This recipe makes quite a bit of peanut butter ganache, but if covered with foil it will keep in the freezer for months.

DR CHUW'S MARZIPAN-STUFFED APRICOTS

As the only recipe in this collection that is not my own creation, Dr Chuw's Marzipan-Stuffed Apricots had to be special if I was willing to put them side-by-side with my own favourites. When Dr Chuw wanted to create a confection that he could present to a confectioner, he came up with a recipe that is both simple and unbelievably delicious. Elegant enough to give to the most discerning of your friends, these apricots are an absolute showstopper.

MAKES 12–24

12–24 whole dried apricots

Marzipan (a small block, to make approximately 45 g (1½ oz) to 90 g (3 oz) of pieces, depending on how full you want your apricots stuffed)

Melted dark chocolate to cover (approximately 90 g/3 oz), or candy coating if preferred

Brandy, if desired (approximately 60 ml/ 2 fl oz to 120 ml/4 fl oz)

1 Gently open all the apricots along their natural seam. It's easiest to open all the apricots before beginning to fill them.

2 Cut small (grape-sized) pieces of marzipan from the block and place inside the apricot. Gently smooth the apricot closed around the marzipan. Allow the marzipan to fill the apricot right up to the edges; this will help to seal the apricot and make for a more attractive confection.

3 Cover in dark chocolate – or candy coating, if you wish – and allow to sit until the chocolate has firmed. This step can be sped up in the refrigerator.

4 Once the chocolates have firmed, they can be wrapped up for gifts. Store in an airtight container in a cool location for up to 2 weeks. Avoid exposure to moist air, as this can make the chocolate grow sticky and 'bloom'.

TIP

For a particularly adult treat, soak the apricots in brandy until they've absorbed all the liquid – between 4 and 12 hours – before stuffing with marzipan. Experiment with other liqueurs for a unique flavour.

CHOCOLATE CHIP COOKIE DOUGH TRUFFLES

For anyone who believes that it is almost a shame to bake cookie dough into its far inferior cookie-form, the chocolate chip cookie dough truffle is a glorious blessing of perfection. The secret is in replacing the eggs with sweetened condensed milk; this gives the truffles all of the great taste of cookie dough with none of the problems with spoiling. I have yet to meet the person who can avoid falling in love after the first bite.

1 Whisk together flour, baking soda and brown sugar until well mixed. Cut in the butter and vanilla until the mixture begins to crumb.

2 Add the condensed milk and stir together, working with your hands as necessary. The dough will be firm and slightly sticky to the touch, but it should not be wet. If it remains too sticky and wet, add more flour 1 tablespoonful at a time.

3 Fold in chocolate chips and nuts, if using, until well blended. Allow to cool until the dough has firmed. This will take several hours in the refrigerator.

4 Using a teaspoon or tablespoon, scoop out a small amount of the dough, depending on the size truffle you prefer. Shape with your hands into a smooth ball (anywhere from marble size to golfball size).

5 Dip in chocolate or candy coating and set aside for several hours until the chocolate has a chance to firm. This can be done in the refrigerator, if you wish.

6 Once the truffles have firmed, they can be wrapped up for gifts. Store in an airtight container in a cool location for up to 2 weeks.

TIP
This dough can be used to bake cookies. Place in a 200°C (390°F) oven for 10 minutes. It can also be adapted to make all of your favourite cookies into truffles. You could replace chocolate chips with dried fruit, or a variety of nuts.

MAKES 12–24

225 g (8 oz) plain flour

1 tsp baking soda (for added flavour)

150 g (5½ oz) packed brown sugar

115 g (4 oz) butter, softened

1 tsp vanilla essence

400-g (14-oz) tin sweetened condensed milk

90 g (3 oz) dark chocolate chips

30 g (1 oz) crushed nuts (optional)

Melted dark, milk or white chocolate to cover (approximately 250 g/9 oz if covering the entire batch), or use candy coating if preferred

STORAGE
This dough freezes very well. Make it in advance or cut the dough into two batches.

FRUITCAKE AND WHITE CHOCOLATE TRUFFLES

When a festive season left behind a surplus of fruitcake and more brandy butter than could be considered seemly, no one was left who could face another bite of this very rich dessert. Clearly, it was time to create a lighter version that had all the flavour of fruitcake, yet with a welcome reduction in holiday heaviness. So delicious, these truffles now come out even in advance of Christmas dinner; this is a fruitcake that makes a very jolly gift.

MAKES 12–24

450 g (16 oz) fruitcake

Brandy butter or plain butter (approximately 4 tbsp)

30 g (1 oz) chopped or crushed nuts (optional)

Thick cream (approximately 4 tbsp)

Melted white chocolate to cover (approximately 250 g/9 oz if covering the full recipe), or use candy coating if preferred

NOTE

If you are using up a portion of leftover cake rather than a whole one, reduce the other ingredients in proportion.

1 Crumble or mash the cake together with the butter until coarsely mixed. Stir in nuts, if using.

2 Stir in the cream until the cake holds its shape when balled together.

3 Allow to cool in the refrigerator until the truffle dough has set up.

4 Using a teaspoon, form balls of the truffle mix, shaping with your hands to the size you prefer.

5 Cover in melted chocolate or candy coating, if using.

6 Allow to harden at room temperature or in refrigerator until set, then pack up in your gift container. Store in an airtight container in a cool location for up to 2 weeks. Avoid exposure to very moist air, as this can make the chocolate grow sticky and 'bloom'.

TIP
This recipe is all about using up your festive leftovers, so it can easily be adapted to what you have to hand. Try using up other treats in a similar fashion. All you need to make a truffle is a cake (without icing) that can be stiffened with a bit of icing or sweetened cream cheese, moistened with cream or butter and then covered in chocolate.

DARK CHOCOLATE AND MARMALADE BARS

A sensible person always keeps on hand a sneakily simple recipe that no one can tell is the go-to easily made gift. This is that recipe for me. Dark chocolate with just a hint of bitterness is always a perfect complement to a deeply citrus marmalade; this recipe allows you to combine the two for a present that will always impress. You can make your own marmalade when time allows, but if you cheat with ready-made, no one will know.

Making the marmalade

1 Using a food processor for speed (this can also be done by hand, if you prefer), first cut the oranges into quarters, and then process until finely chopped. Use the orange peel as your guide to determine if you have achieved fine-cut marmalade or chunkier-peel marmalade. If you do not want much orange rind in your marmalade, partially peel the oranges before processing.

2 Place processed oranges in a saucepan with the sugar and bring to the boil. Keep the mixture bubbling for 20 minutes, until it thickens.

3 Pour into prepared jars. If the jars are sterilised in advance, the marmalade can keep for ages (see page 14 for details). In unsterilised jars, it will keep for several months if kept cool. For this recipe, you'll need only about 115 g (4 oz) marmalade.

Making the chocolate bars

1 Melt two-thirds of the dark chocolate. Add the remaining chocolate to the melted chocolate and stir briskly until it is fully melted (this helps to temper the chocolate and prevents it from blooming as it cools). Pour a thin amount of chocolate into the chocolate bar mould, just enough to cover the bottom.

2 Gently spoon on a thin line of marmalade, being certain that the fruit does not reach the top of the mould. Spoon on melted chocolate to cover the marmalade and completely fill the mould. Be sure that the chocolate, not the marmalade, touches all sides of the mould to keep the marmalade from leaking out. Gently tapping or 'bouncing' the mould on the counter will help to remove any air bubbles.

3 Allow to cool until the chocolate has firmed through. This step can be sped up in the refrigerator. Then pack into gift boxes. Store in an airtight container in a cool location for up to 2 weeks.

MAKES 16 PIECES

MARMALADE
6 oranges

1 kg (2¼ lb) sugar

CHOCOLATE LAYERS
340 g (12 oz) broken or chopped dark chocolate

For these bars you'll need a chocolate mould – I use a 16-bar silicone mould for mine.

VARIATIONS

Try this simple chocolate recipe with the Cranberry and Orange Marmalade found on page 90 – the flavour mix is sensational. Other firm marmalades also do well in chocolate moulds; consider trying lime marmalade or cranberry sauce.

If you want to use a different citrus fruit in your marmalade, be certain that you change the number of fruits so that roughly the same amount of citrus is being used. For example, substitute 2 limes for 1 large orange.

CHAPTER TWO

Chocolate-Covered Cake Bites

Deliciously different, cake bites have all the delights of your favourite cakes but are shaped into bite-sized morsels and enveloped in delicious chocolate. They will keep for one week.

RED VELVET AND CREAM CHEESE CAKE BITES

When I was a young girl, there was no better cake in the world than a red velvet cake. These cake bites bring this treat into bite-sized form.

Making the cake

1 Preheat oven to 180°C (350°F). Grease and flour (or line with parchment paper) a 23x32-cm (9x13-in) tin or two 23-cm (9-in) round cake tins.

2 Sieve the flour and salt into a bowl. Set aside.

3 In a large mixing bowl, whisk together the butter and sugar until they become lightened and fluffy, about 3 minutes. Then begin adding the eggs, beating the mixture and scraping down the sides of the bowl until well combined. Add the vanilla.

4 Add the flour and the soured milk to the butter mixture, in alternating turns. Always begin and end with the flour. Beat until blended.

5 In a small bowl, mix the cocoa and food colouring into a paste. Add this paste to the cake batter and blend well until the batter is incorporated thoroughly.

6 In a small container, mix together the baking soda and vinegar until it foams. Gently fold this into the cake batter by hand. Pour the batter into the prepared tin(s) and bake for 25–30 minutes, until a toothpick inserted in the centre comes out clean. Set aside to cool.

Making the icing

Using an electric whisk, beat together the butter and cream cheese until light and creamy. Add the vanilla and beat well. Mix in the sugar until well incorporated and set aside until ready to use.

Making the cake bites

1 Allow both the cake and the icing to cool completely before working them into balls. Break up the cake into rough crumbs in a bowl that is large enough to work in. It is easier if you use your hands.

2 Mix the icing into the broken-up cake until you have made a dough-like consistency that is like a child's play-dough. Using a melon baller or spoon, shape the cake mixture into balls roughly the size of large marbles or golfballs.

3 Place the formed cake bites onto a plate and chill in the refrigerator for at least 2 hours or overnight. Once they are cooled, melt chocolate or candy coating to cover them. It is helpful to hold the bites on a toothpick or fork in order to dip them in the melted coating. Place each coated bite on a silicone non-stick baking sheet or a plate to allow the coating to set; you can speed up this process, if you want, by putting the cake bites into the refrigerator once they are sticky to the touch. Arrange the bites in a pretty gift package.

MAKES ABOUT 48 BITES

RED VELVET CAKE
300 g (10½ oz) sieved self-raising flour

½ tsp salt

115 g (4 oz) unsalted butter, softened

300 g (10½ oz) granulated sugar

2 eggs

1 tsp vanilla essence

240 ml (8 fl oz) milk mixed with 1 tbsp white vinegar (allow to thicken)

2 heaped tbsp unsweetened cocoa powder

4 tbsp liquid red food colouring

1 tsp white vinegar

1 tsp baking soda

CREAM CHEESE ICING
225 g (8 oz) butter

450 g (16 oz) cream cheese

250 g (9 oz) icing sugar

1 tsp vanilla essence

COATING
About 360 g (12 oz) melted chocolate or candy coating to cover, 180 g (6 oz) of contrasting chocolate to drizzle

CARROT CAKE AND BUTTERCREAM BITES

Carrot cake has that special ability of allowing us to eat cake while we pretend that we are enjoying the healthy benefits of eating our vegetables. These delicious cake bites make an especially beautiful present during the colder months when the spices go so well with warm drinks.

MAKES ABOUT 48 BITES

CARROT CAKE

200 g (7 oz) brown sugar

240 ml (8 fl oz) vegetable oil

3 eggs

3 medium-sized carrots, grated

200 g (7 oz) raisins

Zest of 1 orange

115 g (4 oz) self-raising flour

1 tsp baking soda

1 tsp ground cinnamon

½ tsp ground nutmeg

½ tsp ground cardamom

BUTTERCREAM ICING

225 g (8 oz) butter, softened

190 g (7 oz) icing sugar

1–2 tbsp milk

COATING

About 540 g (1 lb 2 oz) melted white chocolate or candy coating to cover bites

Making the cake

1 Preheat the oven to 180°C (350°F). Grease and flour a 23x32-cm (9x13-in) tin or two 23-cm (9-in) round cake tins.

2 With a spoon, mix together the brown sugar, oil and eggs. Beat lightly with the spoon until the ingredients are well incorporated. Add the grated carrots, raisins and orange zest, and stir through.

3 In a separate bowl, sieve together the flour, baking soda and spices. Gently begin to stir the mixture into the batter until blended through. Stop as soon as the batter is fully mixed together – the batter will be runny and will have some lumps.

4 Pour the batter into the prepared tins and bake for 40–45 minutes, until a toothpick inserted in the centre comes out clean. Set aside to cool.

Making the icing

1 Using an electric whisk, beat the butter until it becomes creamy. Add the sugar by halves, beating it on medium speed until it is smooth.

2 Add 1 tablespoon milk, beat and add more milk as needed until the icing achieves the correct consistency.

3 Set in the refrigerator until ready to use.

Making the cake bites

Follow the instructions on page 43. Cover with several layers of the melted chocolate for a thicker covering. Store in an airtight container in the refrigerator for up to 2 weeks.

TIP
Add an extra spark of orange by using the juice from the orange that you zest for the cake to flavour the icing.

MINT AND CHOCOLATE BITES

There are few flavours as traditionally well-matched with chocolate as the coolness of mint. An infusion of mint in chocolate is both refreshing in the summer and deliciously bracing in colder months.

Making the cake

1. Preheat the oven to 180°C (350°F). Grease and flour a 23x32-cm (9x13-in) tin or two 23-cm (9-in) round cake tins.

2. Sieve together all the dry ingredients into a large bowl until well mixed.

3. In a separate bowl, beat the sugar and shortening together until the mixture is lightened and fluffy. Beat in the egg and peppermint essence until the mixture becomes creamy.

4. Slowly mix in the dry ingredients, alternating with the milk. Beat well throughout.

5. Pour the well-mixed batter into the prepared pans and bake for 25–30 minutes, until a toothpick inserted in the centre comes out clean. Set aside to cool.

Making the icing

1. Cream together the butter and sugar until the mixture is light and fluffy. Add the milk and essence and blend again.

2. Begin mixing the cocoa powder into the butter mixture, beating throughout. If the consistency is wrong, add more milk or sugar until it is right. Set aside until ready to use.

Making the cake bites

Follow the instructions on page 43. Store in an airtight container in the refrigerator for up to 2 weeks.

TIP
If you're looking for a shortcut, you can substitute a devil's food cake mix and add 1–2 teaspoons peppermint essence.

MAKES ABOUT 48 BITES

MINT CAKE
45 g (1½ oz) unsweetened cocoa powder

115 g (4 oz) plain flour

1 tsp baking powder

½ tsp salt

¼ tsp baking soda

150 g (5½ oz) sugar

75 g (2½ oz) butter or shortening

1 egg

1 tsp peppermint essence

160 ml (5½ fl oz) cold milk

CHOCOLATE ICING
6 tbsp butter

340 g (12 oz) icing sugar

5 tbsp milk

1 tsp vanilla or peppermint essence

6 tbsp unsweetened cocoa powder

COATING
About 350 g (12 oz) melted milk chocolate or candy coating to cover, and 180 g (6 oz) of contrasting dark chocolate to drizzle

PEANUT BUTTER AND CHOCOLATE BITES

The taste of salty, rich peanut butter is a wonderful match for the sweet smoothness of chocolate. It's a delicious combination that keeps children happy, yet also manages to be grown-up and tasty enough for adults. Consider making these cake bites when you want to present a crowd-pleasing treat that will be shared with a mixed group; this is one of those taste combinations that many people really love.

MAKES ABOUT 48 BITES

PEANUT BUTTER CAKE
225 g (8 oz) butter, softened

3 tbsp creamy peanut butter

4 eggs

200 g (7 oz) caster or granulated sugar

115 g (4 oz) sour cream or crème fraîche

175 g (6 oz) self-raising flour

CHOCOLATE ICING
See page 47

COATING
About 350 g (12 oz) melted chocolate or candy coating to drizzle over bites

Making the cake

1. Preheat oven to 180°C (350°F). Grease and flour a 23x32-cm (9x13-in) tin or two 20-cm (8-in) round tins.

2. Using an electric whisk, beat together the butter, peanut butter, eggs, sugar and sour cream until the mixture becomes creamy.

3. Fold in the flour and continue to mix together until the batter becomes smooth.

4. Pour the batter into the prepared tin(s) and bake for 30 minutes; when ready, the cake will rise and turn a golden brown and a toothpick inserted in the centre will come out clean. Remove from oven and set aside to cool.

Making the icing

While baking the cake, make the icing. Use the Chocolate Icing from the Mint and Chocolate Bites (page 47). Just make sure you don't add peppermint essence to the chocolate!

Making the cake bites

Follow the instructions on page 43, and decorate. Store in an airtight container in the refrigerator for up to 2 weeks.

TIP
If you buy a ready-made cake, you can use the frosting already on it to make the cake balls – just mix it all together. But if you can find the time to make the cake from scratch, you'll never go back to shop-bought again.

COCONUT AND CREAM CHEESE BITES

With its light, wonderfully subtle taste, coconut perfectly suits being made into a bite-sized treat. For everyone who has ever fallen in love with a coconut chocolate treat, these cake bites bring together that same delicious taste with all that is great about cakes. Make sure you make plenty – these disappear fast.

Making the cake

1 Preheat oven to 180°C (350°F); grease and flour a 23-cm (9-in) round cake tin.

2 Using a wire whisk, mix together the flour, salt and baking powder in a bowl until completely blended together.

3 In a separate bowl, beat together the butter, sugar and egg until well blended and fluffy. Add the vanilla essence.

4 Stir the flour mixture and the milk into the butter mixture, taking turns with each, until well blended and creamy.

5 Fold the coconut through the batter, and when well combined, pour into the prepared tin for baking.

6 Bake for 40 minutes, until a toothpick inserted in the centre comes out clean.

Making the icing

While baking the cake, make the icing. Use the Cream Cheese Icing from the Red Velvet Cake (page 43) for a light, delicious treat.

Making the cake bites

Follow the instructions on page 43, and decorate. Store in an airtight container in the refrigerator for up to 2 weeks.

MAKES ABOUT 24 BITES

COCONUT CAKE
175 g (6 oz) self-raising flour

½ tsp salt

2 tsp baking powder

75 g (2½ oz) butter

65 g (2¼ oz) granulated sugar

1 egg

1 tsp vanilla essence

120 ml (4 fl oz) milk

65 g (2¼ oz) dessicated coconut

CREAM CHEESE ICING
See page 43

COATING
About 250 g (9 oz) melted dark chocolate or candy coating to cover balls

1 tbsp dessicated coconut, to decorate

PUMPKIN CAKE AND SPICED BUTTERCREAM BITES

Pumpkins are a wonderful autumnal vegetable, grossly underrated in baking. The delicious flavours of spiced pumpkin and buttercream combine in this pop-in-the-mouth treat. These cake bites make a perfect present for someone who likes to eat seasonally, or who has a penchant for a spiced carrot cake.

MAKES ABOUT 48 BITES

PUMPKIN CAKE
225 g (8 oz) plain flour

3 tsp baking powder

2 tsp baking soda

¼ tsp salt

2 tsp ground cinnamon

1 tsp ground nutmeg

1 tsp ground cloves

330 g (12 oz) cups superfine or granulated sugar

240 ml (8 fl oz) vegetable oil

425 g (15-oz) tin pumpkin purée (or 500 g/1 lb 2 oz cooked, mashed pumpkin)

4 eggs

BUTTERCREAM ICING
See page 44

COATING
About 500 g (1 lb 2 oz) melted chocolate or candy coating to cover balls

48 shop-bought pumpkin sugar decorations

Making the cake

1. Preheat oven to 180°C (350°F); grease and flour a 23x32-cm (9x13-in) cake tin.

2. Sieve together the flour, baking powder, baking soda, salt and spices into a large bowl.

3. In a separate bowl, combine the sugar and oil, then mix in the pumpkin.

4. Beat in the eggs, one at a time, and then begin to gradually mix in the flour mixture.

5. Pour the batter into the prepared tin and bake for 30-40 minutes, or until the cake is golden brown and a toothpick inserted in the centre comes out clean. Remove the tin from the oven and set aside to cool.

Making the icing

While the cake is baking, make the icing. Use the recipe for the Buttercream Icing from the Carrot Cake (page 44), but flavour the icing with 1 tsp ground cinnamon, ½ tsp ground nutmeg and ½ tsp ground cloves to perfectly complement the pumpkin cake.

Making the cake bites

Follow the instructions on page 43, and decorate. Store in an airtight container in the refrigerator for up to 2 weeks.

LEMON AND CREAM CHEESE CAKE BITES

Lemon and white chocolate make a dreamy combination that manages to be both sweet and tangy, with a luscious creaminess. These dainty little cake bites make a lovely present for any little girl who dreams of growing up and becoming a princess, or for a woman who is perhaps a little older, yet still retains those first romantic dreams. Delicate and ladylike, these are a delightful gift for anyone who likes a very fine dessert.

Making the cake

1 Preheat oven to 180°C (350°F). Grease and flour two 20-cm (8-in) round cake tins.

2 Mix together the melted butter and icing sugar until the sugar is completely incorporated. Whisk in the egg, lemon juice and lemon zest.

3 Sieve the flour into the batter, folding it in gently until well mixed.

4 Pour the batter into the prepared pan and bake for 30 minutes or until a toothpick inserted in the centre comes out clean. Remove the pan from the oven and set aside to cool.

Making the icing

While baking the cake, make the icing and set it aside. The Cream Cheese Icing from the Red Velvet Cake recipe (page 43) is the perfect touch to make this lemon cake into cake bites.

Making the cake bites

Follow the instructions on page 43. Store in an airtight container in the refrigerator for up to 2 weeks.

TIP

Just add a toothpick-tip's amount of yellow food colouring powder or gel (never use liquid food colouring on chocolate as it causes it to seize) and mix well. You can also buy pre-made candy coating in bright yellow colours.

MAKES ABOUT 48 BITES

LEMON CAKE
115 g (4 oz) butter, melted

125 g (4½ oz) icing sugar

1 egg

Juice and zest of 2 lemons

115 g (4 oz) self-raising flour

CREAM CHEESE ICING
See page 43

COATING
About 250 g (9 oz) melted white chocolate to cover the balls, mixed with a drop of yellow food colouring powder or gel

CHAPTER THREE

Soft Treats

Occasionally, one wants something soft and sweet that doesn't let chocolate steal the spotlight. This chapter includes delicious soft treats with indulgent, gourmet touches that make fabulous gifts.

POMEGRANATE CUPCAKES WITH HONEY BUTTERCREAM ICING

Pomegranate molasses is a revelation — such an intensely sharp, flavourful syrup just begs to be used in myriad ways. Where it really comes into its own is when it elevates a light and delicious cupcake.

Making the cupcakes

1 Preheat the oven to 190°C (375°F). Place paper or silicone cupcake liners in 1 or 2 muffin tins, depending on the size you want your cupcakes.

2 Beat the softened butter until it starts to lighten; the butter will begin to 'fluff up' and increase in size slightly.

3 In a separate bowl, whisk the dry ingredients until well mixed. Mix the milk and eggs together.

4 Mix the dry ingredients, alternating with the milk and eggs, into the whipped butter. Beat well until you have a soft batter. Fold the pomegranate molasses and pomegranate seeds gently into the batter until they are well incorporated.

5 Pour the batter into cupcake liners, filling each to no more than ⅔ full. Bake for approximately 15 minutes, until the cupcakes are raised and just starting to brown. Set aside and allow to cool before icing them.

Making the buttercream icing

1 Whip the butter until lightened. Beat in the sugar. Beat the mixture hard until it is light and fluffy, becoming a stiff mixture that holds its shape.

2 Mix in the honey or golden syrup and give a final beating; adjust the honey or syrup to give you the desired consistency and flavour. Allow to cool in the refrigerator before applying to the cooled cupcakes.

3 Arrange your cupcakes in your gift box. Store in an airtight container in the refrigerator for up to 2 days, or freeze in a sealed container for up to 2 weeks.

TIP
Impress your friends by making two special flavours of cupcakes without making any extra work for yourself. You could make the basic batter mix and add the seeds of 1 pomegranate and half of the molasses to one half of the batter, reserving the other half of batter for another flavour.

MAKES 12–24 CUPCAKES

CUPCAKES
145 g (5 oz) unsalted butter, softened

190 g (6½ oz) caster sugar

145 g (5 oz) self-raising flour

Pinch salt

4 eggs

4 tbsp low-fat milk

120 ml (4 fl oz) pomegranate molasses

Seeds from 2 fresh pomegranates

HONEY BUTTERCREAM
75 g (2½ oz) unsalted butter, softened

600 g (1 lb 5 oz) icing sugar, sieved

60–120 ml (2–4 fl oz) honey (or light golden syrup, if preferred)

TIP
Increasing the honey allows for a runnier icing, if you want to pour it on. Use less if you want to spread or pipe on the icing.

REDCURRANT CUPCAKES WITH WHITE CHOCOLATE ICING

There are few things that can top fresh redcurrants when it comes to instilling instant cheer. Naturally tart, yet with a lighter sweetness than you find in cranberries, the redcurrant marries perfectly with white chocolate to create a very grown-up taste. These cupcakes are light and moist, and will please even the most discerning cupcake fan.

MAKES 12–24 CUPCAKES

CUPCAKES

275 g (9¼ oz) unsalted butter, softened

190 g (7 oz) caster sugar

145 g (5 oz) self-raising flour

Pinch salt

4 eggs

4 tbsp low-fat milk

300 g (10½ oz) fresh redcurrants (approximately)

250 g (9 oz) broken or chopped white chocolate

WHITE CHOCOLATE BUTTERCREAM

75 g (2½ oz) unsalted butter, softened

625 g (1 lb 5 oz) icing sugar, sieved

175 g (6 oz) melted white chocolate, cooled to room temperature

Making the cupcakes

1 Preheat the oven to 190°C (375°F). Place paper cupcake liners in 1 or 2 muffin tins, depending on the size you want your cupcakes.

2 Beat the softened butter until it starts to lighten; the butter will begin to 'fluff up' and increase in size slightly.

3 Whisk together the dry ingredients until well mixed.

4 Mix the eggs and milk together.

5 Mix the dry ingredients, alternating with the milk and eggs, into the whipped butter. Beat well until you have a soft batter. Fold the redcurrants and melted white chocolate gently into the batter until they are mixed through.

6 Pour the batter into prepared muffin cups, filling each to no more than ⅔ full. Bake for approximately 15 minutes, until the cakes are raised and just starting to brown. Set aside and allow to cool before icing the cakes.

Making the buttercream icing

1 Whip the butter until lightened.

2 Beat in the sugar. Beat the mixture hard until it is light and fluffy, becoming a stiff mixture that holds its shape.

3 Mix in the melted white chocolate and give a final beating. Allow to cool in the refrigerator before applying to the cooled cupcakes.

4 Pack your cupcakes in your gift box. Store in an airtight container in the refrigerator for up to 2 days, or freeze in a sealed container for up to 2 weeks.

TRIPLE CHOCOLATE BROWNIES

Just about everyone loves brownies; with all the best features of chocolate cake and soft biscuits, brownies manage to combine the best of both worlds. You can hardly swing a cat without coming across any old standard brownie recipe or box mix. What makes these brownies special enough to warrant being made into a very impressive gift for that special someone is a trio of chocolates. Milk, dark and white chocolate together make for a chocolate-lover's dream come true.

1 Preheat oven to 180°C (350°F). Grease and flour a 23x32-cm (9x13-in) tin (or smaller if you want thicker brownies).

2 Whisk together cocoa and baking soda until well blended. Mix in 80 ml (3 fl oz) oil and the hot water until well mixed. Add the sugar and eggs and mix again. Stir in the flour and salt until wet through. Then add the vanilla and remaining 80 ml (3 fl oz) oil, and stir until blended.

3 Stir in the chocolate pieces, then immediately pour batter into prepared tin and bake for 30–45 minutes. The cooking time depends very much upon your oven and how dry you like your brownies. I bake mine for just under 25 minutes because I like very moist brownies. For more cake-like brownies, cook for 25–30 minutes.

4 Let brownies cool, then cut into pieces and arrange in your gift package. Store in an airtight container for up to 3 days, or freeze in a sealed container for up to 2 weeks.

MAKES 1 TIN BROWNIES

75 g (2½ oz) unsweetened cocoa powder

½ heaped tsp baking soda

160 ml (6 fl oz) vegetable oil

120 ml (4 fl oz) hot water

200 g (7 oz) granulated sugar

2 eggs

175 g (6 oz) plain flour

¼ tsp salt

1 tsp vanilla essence

175 g (6 oz) (total) equal proportions of white, dark and milk chocolate chips or pieces

TIP

Put your chocolate chips or pieces into the freezer before you use them. That way they don't fully melt into the brownie, so you end up with little pockets of perfect chocolatey goodness.

MAPLE SYRUP CUPCAKES WITH WALNUT BUTTERCREAM ICING

This is a cake for the colder seasons and tucking up around the fire after crunching through the changing leaves in the brisk autumn weather.

MAKES 12–18 CUPCAKES

CUPCAKES

290 g (10 oz) plain flour

2 tsp baking powder

1 tsp baking soda

½ tsp salt

1 tsp ground cinnamon

115 g (4 oz) butter, softened

100 g (3½ oz) brown sugar

2 eggs

300 ml (10 fl oz) maple syrup

2 tsp vanilla essence

120 ml (4 fl oz) milk mixed with 1 tbsp vinegar; let sit until thickened and soured

WALNUT BUTTERCREAM

75 g (2½ oz) unsalted butter, softened

625 g (1 lb 5 oz) icing sugar, sieved

1 tsp walnut essence (optional)

45 g (1½ oz) crushed toasted walnuts

Making the cupcakes

1. Preheat oven to 180°C (350°F). Prepare 1½ regular-size muffin tins or 1 large muffin tin, using cupcake liners or silicone cups.

2. Using a whisk, mix together all the dry ingredients in a large bowl until they are well incorporated. It is especially important that the baking soda and powder are well mixed through; this is what makes the cupcakes fluffy.

3. In another large bowl, beat together the butter and brown sugar until the colour lightens and the consistency becomes creamy. Add the eggs, maple syrup and vanilla to the butter and sugar mixture. Blend with an electric whisk on a medium speed until the batter is smooth and consistent.

4. Blend the flour mixture, alternating with the soured milk mixture, into the batter, beginning and ending with the flour mixture. Pour the batter into prepared muffin tins, ensuring that each cup is filled no more than ⅔ full.

5. Bake for 20–22 minutes; touch a spoon to the top of a cupcake to see if it is bouncy (the spoon indentation will spring back when released). If you insert a toothpick into the centre of a cupcake, it should come out clean. Allow the cupcakes to cool fully before icing.

Making the buttercream icing

1. Whip the butter until lightened. Beat in the sugar. Beat the mixture hard until it is light and fluffy, becoming a stiff mixture that holds its shape. Blend in the walnut essence, if using.

2. Mix in the crushed walnuts and stir well. Apply icing generously to the cooled cupcakes. Pack up cupcakes in your gift container. Store in an airtight container in the refrigerator for up to 2 days, or freeze in a sealed container for up to 2 weeks.

CINNAMON AND TOFFEE CUPCAKES

When these flavours are combined in the form of a moist and delicious cupcake, it's an ideal treat to give to someone you care about.

Making the toffee

1. Pour the sugar into a saucepan over medium heat and stir briskly as the sugar melts. Continue stirring to prevent scorching until the sugar has completely melted and begins to boil. As soon as you see it bubbling along the sides, stop stirring.

2. Watch for the melted sugar to become a dark amber colour; when this happens, add the butter. Whisk the mixture briskly until the butter melts into the sugar. When it is fully incorporated, remove from the heat.

3. With the pan off the heat, stir through 3 times, then begin to slowly pour in the whipping cream. Whisk the mixture constantly until it is creamy and the cream is completely blended in.

4. Pour the cooling mixture into several heavy-duty jars and allow to fully cool before handling. Remember that sugar boils at a very high heat and will stick to your skin – avoid contact until the sides of the jars are cool to the touch. (I use several jars to help the toffee to cool faster, and I do not use all the toffee in one cupcake recipe.)

Making the cupcakes

1. Preheat oven to 180°C (350°F). Place cupcake liners into 9 large or 18 regular-sized muffin cups.

2. Blend all the dry ingredients – flour, baking powder, baking soda, cinnamon and salt – in a bowl until well mixed. Ensure that the ingredients are fully incorporated, as the baking powder and soda need to be evenly distributed to ensure that the cupcakes rise.

3. In a large bowl, beat together the softened butter and the sugar, until the mixture begins to lighten and has a soft, creamy consistency. Mix the eggs and the sour cream into the butter mixture until the batter becomes well blended and creamy.

4. Stir in the flour and toffee mixtures in alternating batches, beginning and ending with the flour mixture, and using as much of the toffee as desired. Pour the batter into prepared cupcake liners, ensuring that each is filled no more than ⅔ full. Bake for 20–25 minutes or until the cupcakes spring back when pressed with the back of a spoon. Ice with buttercream icing. (The icing on page 62 is a good option; just omit the walnuts and walnut essence and flavour with cinnamon instead.) Store in an airtight container in the refrigerator for up to 2 days, or freeze in a sealed container for up to 2 weeks.

MAKES 9–18 CUPCAKES

TOFFEE

200 g (7 oz) sugar

6 tbsp butter

120 ml (4 fl oz) double or whipping cream

CUPCAKES

225 g (8 oz) plain flour

1½ tsp baking powder

½ tsp baking soda

2 tsp ground cinnamon

½ tsp salt

175 g (6 oz) unsalted butter, softened

125 g (4½ oz) granulated sugar

2 eggs

150 g (5½ oz) sour cream or fromage frais

BUTTERCREAM

625 g (1 lb 5 oz) icing sugar, sieved

75 g (2½ oz) unsalted butter, softened

½ tsp cinnamon

TIP

Have everything ready for the syrup before you begin. The mixture will rise up when you add the cream.

HONEY TARTS

Throughout history, honey has been used for its medicinal and sweetening properties. It has also been recognised for its religious and symbolic qualities. There is no surprise, then, that honey is loved the world over. With a crumbly (though surprisingly simple) pastry and creamy sweet filling, this is one tart that will make a wonderfully tempting present.

MAKES 24 MINI OR 12 SMALL TARTS

PASTRY

115 g (4 oz) plain flour

50 g (1¾ oz) brown sugar

50 g (1¾ oz) chopped pecans

115 g (4 oz) butter, melted

FILLING

200 g (7 oz) brown sugar

120 ml (4 fl oz) water

1 egg, beaten

1½ tbsp honey

¼ tsp ground nutmeg

¼ tsp ground allspice

¼ tsp ground cinnamon

25 g (1 oz) crushed or whole pecans (optional)

Making the pastry

1 Whisk together the flour, brown sugar and nuts until well blended.

2 Add the melted butter and stir together until you can form a ball. You can add more flour if the mixture becomes too wet to handle; however, the pastry does not have to be perfectly workable, as you will be forming it in the tartlet pans rather than rolling it out.

3 Divide the dough into small balls – 24 balls if using very small tartlet pans, or 12 if using larger pans. Gently press and work the dough to the edges of the pan with your fingertips.

4 Chill the prepared pastry while you work on the filling. This pastry is not blind-baked before adding the filling.

Making the filling

1 Preheat the oven to 200°C (400°F).

2 Boil the brown sugar and water until it forms a light syrup (bring just to the boil and allow to incorporate, but do not continue to boil past that point). Remove from heat and allow to cool.

3 Add the eggs, honey and spices, and beat thoroughly. Pour the mixture into the unbaked pastry, filling the pie pan or tart shells no more than ⅔ full. Sprinkle the pie or tarts with crushed or whole pecans if desired and bake for 20 minutes.

4 Remove from the oven and let cool. Store in an airtight container for up to a week.

TIP
Use this recipe to make 1 large tart for a party – it makes a beautiful dessert.

MARSHMALLOWS

If you are convinced that marshmallows are boring and rightfully overlooked, then you have never had the opportunity to try the magic that is a homemade marshmallow. With a texture that is silky smooth and a taste that is divine, marshmallows make a wonderful treat on their own or when used to dress up hot drinks and desserts.

[1] In the bowl of an electric whisk, sprinkle gelatin over 120 ml (4 fl oz) cold water. Soak for 10 minutes.

[2] Combine sugar, golden syrup and remaining 60 ml (2 fl oz) water in a small saucepan. Bring to the boil and boil hard for 1 minute. Pour boiling syrup into gelatin and mix at high speed with an electric whisk.

[3] Add the salt and beat for 12 minutes. The mixture will be doubled in size and have turned white – this can sometimes take longer depending on your individual kitchen's variables, so keep beating until it does happen. Add vanilla and incorporate into the mixture.

[4] Scrape the mixture into a tin lined with oiled clingfilm. A silicone non-stick baking sheet found in cooking shops is terrific when it comes to working with your cooled marshmallows. A 23x23-cm (9x9-in) tin or a 23x32-cm (9x13-in) tin will work fine; choose the size you want based on how thick you want your marshmallows to be. Spread out evenly. (Lightly oil hands and spatula or bowl scraper.)

[5] Lightly sprinkle the top of the marshmallow mixture with the mixture of icing sugar and cream of tartar. Let the mixture sit for a few hours, cooling in the refrigerator if it is warm. This process may take from 5 hours to overnight.

[6] Remove the marshmallow slab gently from the pan, dredging it with icing sugar as you work. Cut the marshmallow into the desired-sized pieces (I use kitchen shears as my preference, but some people prefer to use a knife). Dredge the sides of each piece of marshmallow in a mixture of icing sugar and cream of tartar.

[7] Your marshmallows are now ready to wrap and gift. Store in an airtight container (avoiding extremes in humidity) for up to 3 months.

MAKES ABOUT 12

3 packets unflavoured gelatin

180 ml (6 fl oz) cold water

400 g (14 oz) granulated sugar

160 ml (6 fl oz) light golden syrup

60 ml (2 fl oz) water

¼ tsp salt

1 tbsp vanilla essence

Icing sugar and cream of tartar, for dredging (a 50:50 ratio, or more sugar if desired)

TIP

Add different flavours to your marshmallow mixture to make wonderfully unique gifts – try mint for adding to steaming mugs of cocoa or nutmeg and pumpkin spice to enjoy with coffee.

CHAPTER FOUR

Candies and Fudges

Here are recipes for delicious sweet treats that are waiting to be boxed up and presented to the delight of your friends and family. Whether you're looking for a traditional confectionary or a new take on an old classic, this chapter will show you how to make the perfect gift.

BROWN SUGAR AND BUTTER MAGIC BRITTLE

When I told a friend who had once received this brittle from me that this recipe was going in the book, he said the only problem would be that there is no real way to convey in writing the deliciousness of this brittle. I can only try to tell you that you will never find an easier-to-make, tastier brittle.

1 Preheat oven to 200°C (400°F); grease or line a sheet pan with foil or a non-stick baking sheet.

2 Cover the prepared sheet with half of the crackers.

3 Melt the butter in a saucepan. Add the brown sugar and bring to the boil. Allow to boil gently – stirring continuously – until the sugar and butter are completely incorporated. This will take about 6 minutes; the mixture will become a lighter brown and will begin to fluff up.

4 Remove from the heat and immediately stir in the baking powder until fully mixed. The mixture will fluff further.

5 Pour half of the mixture over the crackers in the pan; line it with the remaining crackers and cover with the remaining mixture.

6 Bake in the oven for 6 minutes.

7 Remove from the oven and sprinkle the chocolate over the top. Leave the chocolate to soften from the heat of the brittle for a couple of minutes, then spread it gently with a spatula.

8 Let the brittle cool before breaking it into pieces and placing them in a gift package. Store in an airtight container in a cool location for up to 1 week.

MAKES ABOUT 450 GRAMS (1 POUND)

18 cream crackers

225 g (8 oz) butter

100 g (3½ oz) brown sugar

½ tsp baking powder

175 g (6 oz) dark chocolate chips or small chocolate pieces

TIP
Never, ever, forget to grease your pan before preparing this treat; alternatively use a silicone non-stick baking sheet in the pan. If you let the brittle cool completely before loosening it in the pan, it becomes incredibly difficult to get out.

MACADAMIA AND PEANUT BRITTLE

Known for being wonderfully crunchy, this brittle manages to be just the right mix of toffee and salty nuts – it makes a wonderful present, no matter what time of year.

MAKES ABOUT 450 GRAMS (1 POUND)

100 g (3½ oz) white sugar

120 ml (4 fl oz) light golden syrup

¼ tsp salt

60 ml (2 fl oz) water

75 g (2½ oz) peanuts

60 g (2 oz) macadamia nuts

2 tbsp butter, softened

1 tsp baking soda

VARIATIONS
Try your own favourite nuts in this recipe; for instance, add Brazil nuts and cover with chocolate for a special treat.

1 Grease a large baking sheet and set it aside, or place a silicone non-stick baking sheet on the counter.

2 In a heavy-bottomed 2-litre (3½-pint) saucepan, mix together the sugar, golden syrup, salt and water. Add a sugar thermometer, if you have one, to the pan. Bring the mixture to the boil and allow it to remain boiling throughout.

3 As soon as the mixture begins to boil, add the nuts.

4 It is important to stir steadily throughout the cooking process – keep the stirring slow and steady, as too rapid a stir will slow down the temperature increase, but not stirring will allow the sugar to burn on the bottom.

5 Boil the sugar mixture until it reaches 150°C (300°F), or until it reaches hard crack stage (a small amount dropped into very cold water will separate and form hard, brittle threads).

6 When the sugar mixture reaches the right temperature, immediately remove the pan from the heat and add the butter. Stir until melted. Add the baking soda. It will fluff up; stir gently to mix through.

7 Pour the mixture out onto the prepared sheet, using the back of a spoon to spread it evenly. Allow the brittle to cool completely before breaking into pieces and placing in a gift package. Store in an airtight container, completely free from moisture, for up to 3 months.

TIP
This recipe moves fast; make sure you have your baking soda and butter already measured out before you begin.

POMEGRANATE MOLASSES CHEWS

*When I needed a present for a man with a devilishly particular palate,
I turned to a bottle of thick, tart pomegranate molasses to create a sweet that
was as unctuous and delicious as a caramel chew, but had a more
exotic and unusual flavour.*

1 Prepare a 23-cm (9-in) tin in advance by greasing it or by lining it with aluminium foil or a non-stick baking sheet.

2 Put all of the ingredients in a heavy-bottomed saucepan over a medium heat. As the mixture warms, stir it continually to help the ingredients incorporate.

3 Place a sugar thermometer in the tin and bring the mixture to the boil. Leave it on a steady heat and bring the sugar temperature up to 150°C (280°F). Be sure to stir regularly through this process so that the mixture does not burn. This will take roughly 15–20 minutes. Be very careful to watch it closely towards the end of the time; the temperature will rise surprisingly fast as it gets close to done.

4 As soon as the mixture reaches 150°C (280°F), remove it from the heat and pour it into the prepared tin.

5 Allow to cool for a few minutes until the mixture begins to harden slightly; at this point, score across the top to make it easier to separate into pieces. When the toffee has fully cooled, it can be snapped along these lines.

6 Pack the cooled molasses in an airtight gift container, as moisture can make the candy soften. Store in an airtight container, completely free from moisture, for up to 3 months.

**MAKES ABOUT
450 GRAMS
(1 POUND)**

250 g (9 oz) granulated sugar

60 ml (2 fl oz) water

1 tbsp light golden syrup

3 tbsp pomegranate molasses

7 tbsp butter

TIP
Pomegranate molasses is popular in Lebanese and Middle Eastern cooking. You can find it in most speciality and healthfood shops.

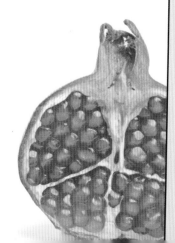

DARK MOLASSES TOFFEE

After moving abroad from the United States, I found that one taste that was incredibly hard to find was the rich complexity of a dark molasses toffee; I simply had to find a way to make it at home. Dark molasses imbues a flavour that is as dark as its name and has a unique depth, which walks the line between sweet and sharp.

MAKES ABOUT 450 GRAMS (1 POUND)

250 g (9 oz) dark brown sugar

60 ml (2 fl oz) water

1 tbsp light golden syrup

3 tbsp molasses

7 tbsp butter

1. Prepare a 23-cm (9-in) tin in advance by greasing it or by lining it with aluminium foil or a non-stick baking sheet.

2. Put all of the ingredients in a heavy-bottomed saucepan over a medium heat. As the mixture heats up, stir it continually to help it incorporate.

3. Place a sugar thermometer in the pan and bring the mixture to a boil. Leave it on a steady heat and bring the temperature up to 150°C (300°F). Be sure to stir regularly through this process so that the mixture does not burn. This will take roughly 15–20 minutes. Be very careful to watch it closely toward the end of the time, because the temperature will rise surprisingly quickly as it gets close to done.

4. As soon as the mixture reaches the final temperature, remove it from the heat and pour it into the prepared tin.

5. Allow the molasses to cool for a few minutes until it begins to harden slightly; at this point, score across the top to make it easier to separate into pieces. When the toffee has fully cooled, it can be snapped along these lines.

6. Pack the cooled toffee in an airtight gift container, as moisture can make the toffee soften. Store in an airtight container, completely free from moisture, for up to 3 months.

TIP

Toffees and chews change according to how hot you let their sugar mixture get. A brittle toffee recipe can easily become a soft dark chew if you remove it from the heat when it reaches the firm ball stage rather than the hard crack stage.

MINT AND CHOCOLATE FUDGE

Chocolate fudge can be almost too richly decadent at times; fortunately, however, the cool sharpness of mint cuts through that sweetness. With its velvety smooth texture and a rapturous melding of mint and chocolate, this fudge is infinitely luxurious as a present.

1. Prepare a 20-cm (8-in) tin by greasing and flouring it, or by lining it with parchment paper or a non-stick baking sheet.

2. In a heavy-bottomed saucepan, melt the dark chocolate with 240 ml (8 fl oz) of the condensed milk and the vanilla essence over a low heat. Remove from the heat as soon as the chocolate has melted.

3. At the same time, in a second saucepan, melt the white chocolate and the remaining condensed milk with the peppermint essence. Remove from the heat as soon as the white chocolate has melted. (You prepare the two parts separately because of the difference in how long it takes the two types of chocolate to melt.)

5. Stir the melted white chocolate mixture into the dark chocolate mixture. Pour the combined mixture into the prepared pan.

6. Allow to set firmly, at least 4 hours or overnight in the refrigerator. Cut into pieces or wrap as a gift.

7. Store in an airtight container for up to 3 weeks.

MAKES ABOUT 450 GRAMS (1 POUND)

350 g (12 oz) dark chocolate chips

400 g (14-oz) tin sweetened condensed milk, divided

2 tsp vanilla essence

175 g (6 oz) white chocolate chips or broken pieces

1 tbsp peppermint essence

TIP

If you like a more dramatic presentation, you can make this in layers. Simply pour the dark chocolate portion in the tin and allow it to set partially before preparing the white chocolate portion. When making the white chocolate, add a few drops of green food colouring at the final moment. Then pour the entire batch over the dark chocolate. Set in the fridge until firm.

WHITE CHOCOLATE AND BLUEBERRY FUDGE

This fudge started out as a truffle. I was wanting to find a way to make a delicious white chocolate candy and discovered that I could make a silky ganache pegged with lush dried blueberries. It was so tasty, in fact, that everyone wanted it in larger pieces as a fudge. The blueberries give it a taste of summer, but there is no time when this doesn't make a wonderful gift.

MAKES ABOUT 450 GRAMS (1 POUND)

200 g (9 oz) caster or granulated sugar

1½ tbsp butter

¼ tsp salt

120 ml (4 fl oz) sweetened condensed milk

1 tsp vanilla essence

250 g (9 oz) chopped white chocolate

125 g (4½ oz) dried blueberries

1. Grease a 23-cm (9-in) baking tin.

2. Put the sugar, butter, salt, milk and vanilla in a heavy-bottomed saucepan. Bring the mixture to the boil over medium heat, being very careful to stir it throughout so that it does not scald. Lower the heat after the mixture reaches boiling point, and simmer for 5 minutes, while continuing to stir.

3. Remove from the heat and add the chocolate pieces. Allow the heat to permeate the chocolate for a few moments before stirring to incorporate. When the chocolate has melted into the mixture, stir in the blueberries.

4. Pour the mixture into the prepared tin and place it in the refrigerator. The fudge will need at least 4 hours and preferably overnight in the refrigerator to fully set.

5. Cut into pieces to serve or wrap as a gift. Store in an airtight container for up to 3 weeks, or freeze in a sealed container for up to 3 months. Avoid moisture and extremes in temperature.

TIP

Try this recipe with other richly flavoured dried fruits – cranberries and cherries are both especially delicious.

PEPPERMINT CREAMS

Peppermint creams are a decadent little treat that are surprisingly easy to make at home, but anyone who is lucky enough to receive these will be convinced you are an absolute angel in the kitchen. Pairing an icy peppermint filling with dark, nearly bitter chocolate is an ideal taste combination. These creams put you in mind of a bracing alpine winter spent skiing and warming up by the fire – even if you've never set foot in snow.

1. Mix the condensed milk, peppermint essence and icing sugar in a large bowl. This will form a very stiff dough, which will require quite a bit of 'working' with your hands until it is smooth. The final dough should be firm and not sticky. Add additional sugar or milk to get the right consistency.

2. With a rolling pin, roll out the dough about 5-mm to 1-cm (¼ to ½-in) thick (dusting the rolling pin with sugar will prevent it from sticking). Cut out the shapes that you want. This can either be simple squares or use a small glass to make circles.

3. Set out the creams to dry on non-stick baking sheets. Let them dry for several hours on each side until they are firm enough to work with. This may take as long as 12 hours.

4. Once the creams have dried, pour the melted chocolate into a bowl. Drop in a cream, flip it over to coat, and bring it out with a fork or spoon. Lay it on the baking sheet and repeat with the remaining confectionary.

5. Place the creams in the refrigerator to set. This may take about 2 hours.

6. Arrange in a gift box. Store in an airtight container for up to 2 weeks.

TIP
This is such a simple recipe that it suits adaptation with other flavours. Try replacing the peppermint essence with cherry flavouring or orange essence.

MAKES ABOUT 48 2-CM (1-IN) CREAMS

180 ml (6 fl oz) sweetened condensed milk

2½ tsp peppermint essence

495 g (1 lb 1 oz) icing sugar (1 full 500-g/17-oz box, minus about a tablespoon)

About 175 g (6 oz) melted dark chocolate to cover

CHAPTER FIVE

Preserves and Jellies

One of the best-kept secrets of the cooking world is just how easy it is to make jams, jellies and marmalades. Whip up a small batch of handmade, stunningly flavoured preserves and impress your loved ones.

APPLE BUTTER

Fruit butters are one of the best ways to use up a bumper harvest of fruit and ensure that there is a richly flavoured, healthy spread available to get you through cooler autumn mornings. Don't be fooled by the name – there is no butter of any kind in this spread. The name comes from its thick, rich, spreadable texture. This recipe was my grandfather's favourite, especially when spread on thick homemade buttered bread.

1 Clean and core the apples, cutting them roughly into chunks. Do not peel.

2 Place the apple pieces into a slow cooker with the water or juice; you need only enough water or juice to keep the apples moist while they cook down. Cover and let cook in the slow cooker on a low temperature for 12 hours or overnight.

3 For rustic apple butter, process the cooked apples using a hand blender until smooth; if desired, put the apples through a food mill at this point to completely remove the peel.

4 Sweeten and spice the apple butter – the amount should be roughly 200 g (7 oz) sugar, 1 teaspoon cinnamon and ½ teaspoon each of cloves and allspice for each 275 g (9½ oz) of apples. This is very much to taste, however, so do make adaptations.

5 Raise the temperature to high and continue to cook for an additional 4–6 hours (with the final 2–3 hours done with the lid off the slow cooker), until the apple butter is thick enough to remain on the spoon when turned over.

6 Spoon into sterilised jars and seal (see page 14 for details). Unsealed or unprocessed jars of apple butter will be perfectly fine in the refrigerator for up to 3 weeks; processed and sterile jars will keep for up to a year in the cupboard until opened.

MAKES ABOUT 1–1½ LITRES (2–3 PINTS)

10–15 sweet apples (the number depends on the size of your slow cooker and the size of the apples; use the number that fit comfortably in the pot)

120–240 ml (4–8 fl oz) water or apple juice

200–600 g (7 oz–1 lb 5 oz) sugar

Ground cinnamon

Ground cloves

Ground allspice

TIP
This recipe can be easily adapted to change the amount of butter that you make; just keep everything roughly in proportion.

APPLE AND CHILLI JELLY

The beauty of this jelly is in the unexpected tickle of warm chilli flavour combined with the sweet lightness of apples. It works equally well as a breakfast toast accompaniment or as a delicious contrast to a sharp cheddar cheese as a savoury snack.

MAKES ABOUT 1½ LITRES (3 PINTS)

1½–1¾ litres (2½– 2¾ pints) pure apple juice

1 packet dry pectin or 1 bottle liquid pectin

1½ kg (3 lb) sugar (this amount can be halved – or replaced with sweetener – if you increase the amount of pectin)

3–5 chillies, finely chopped

1 Pour the apple juice into a large kettle. If using liquid pectin, mix it with the apple juice and bring to the boil on the stove. If using dry pectin, mix the dry pectin with 50 g (1¾ oz) of sugar, and then mix it with the juice and bring to the boil.

2 Once the juice has come to the boil, mix in the remaining sugar and continue boiling. Boil hard for 2–3 minutes.

3 Stir in the chopped chillies and pour the juice into prepared sterilised jars (see page 14 for details).

4 While the jelly is setting, turn the jars upside down to ensure that the chillies do not collect on the bottom. Five minutes upright and then 5 minutes flipped over should allow the jelly to set and keep the chillies floating. Once the jelly is set, it is ready to store. It can be kept for several weeks in the refrigerator as is. If the jars are sterilised and sealed, it can be kept for months in the cupboard.

TIP
Using pure fruit juice is the absolute best way to 'cheat' your way to easy jams – it allows you to make any jam without first processing raw fruit. Just be sure to allow for enough added pectin to account for the reduction in natural pectin that you get when working with ripe fruit.

POMEGRANATE JAM

Pomegranates have a place in the hearts of food lovers who appreciate the tart ruby red seeds for their healthy super-food status. Beyond the nutritional value, however, is the delicious grown-up flavour that evokes all the mystery of Greek mythology and the romance of faraway lands.

1. Bring juice to the boil; add sugar and pectin or gelatin. Allow to boil hard for 2 minutes.

2. Stir in pomegranate molasses and remove from heat.

3. Skim off any foam and pour into prepared jars (see page 14 for details). Store in a sterilised jar in a cool, dark cupboard for up to 2 years. Check the seal on the jar before eating anything that has been stored for more than a month; the lid should be firm with no gaps in the seal.

MAKES 1½ LITRES (3 PINTS)

1 litre (1¾ pints) pure pomegranate juice

400 g (14 oz) sugar

1 packet dry pectin

120 ml (4 fl oz) pomegranate molasses

VARIATION
Replace 240 ml (8 fl oz) of juice with the juice and seeds of 2 or 3 pomegranates for a more textured jelly; try this jelly as a replacement for cranberry sauce with poultry.

TIP
You can make this jelly more tart by using just 200 g (7 oz) sugar and 1 packet unflavoured gelatin (instead of pectin), if desired.

CRANBERRY AND ORANGE MARMALADE

Cranberries and oranges are both evocative of the warmth of holiday festivities snuggled in tight from the chill of winter. When these flavours are brought together, the result is a richly sweet and tart marmalade that mingles wonderfully with gingerbread, fruitcake and all the deliciousness of wintertime treats. Presenting this marmalade as a gift will be as welcome as the comfort of woollen scarves and mittens on a frosty winter morning.

MAKES ABOUT 1–1½ LITRES (2–3 PINTS)

480 ml (16 fl oz) water, divided (if using whole oranges), or 120 ml (4 fl oz) water (if using marmalade)

600 g (1 lb 5 oz) sugar, divided (if using whole oranges), or 200 g (7 oz) sugar (if using marmalade)

1 tsp ground cloves

125 g (4½ oz) cranberries, fresh or frozen

6 whole oranges or 1 kg (2½ lb) ready-made orange marmalade

120 ml (4 fl oz) Grand Marnier (optional)

Orange rind (if using prepared marmalade)

1 Boil 120 ml (4 fl oz) water with 200 g (7 oz) sugar and the cloves until the sugar is melted. Add cranberries and allow to remain on the boil for approximately 30 minutes, until the cranberries have puffed up and become soft. They should not be breaking and turning to mush, however; remove pan from heat and set aside.

2 To prepare the marmalade if not using ready-made: Peel and section the oranges, collecting the rind from 3 of the oranges. Be sure to not get any of the white pith when preparing the oranges, as this will make the marmalade bitter. Add the oranges to 360 ml (12 fl oz) of water and 400 g (14 oz) of sugar, and bring to the boil. Add the Grand Marnier if using, and allow to remain at boiling point until the mixture reaches the jelly stage (this is at 110°C/220°F), usually 20–25 minutes.

3 If using ready-made marmalade: Put marmalade, additional orange rind if desired and Grand Marnier (if using) in a pot, and bring to the boil. Allow to boil for 20–25 minutes until the mixture reaches the jelly stage.

4 Remove the cranberries from the excess liquid and mix gently with the marmalade. Bring back to a boil and then reduce heat to a simmer. Allow to simmer for 5 minutes before pouring into prepared jars (see page 14 for details). Store in a sterilised jar in a cool, dark cupboard for up to 2 years.

LEMON CURD

Tangy, zesty lemon curd makes a wonderful palate-cleansing dessert. Give someone a jar of lemon curd as a gift and they can bake it into their own lemon meringue pie or into little tarts, but they are just as likely to eat it right out of the jar or spread it on toast. This wonderful treat is so delicious and so versatile; it certainly won't hang around for long.

1 Lightly whisk the eggs in a large saucepan.

2 Put all other ingredients in the pan with the eggs and mix together briskly until well blended, adding the lemon juice and zest last.

3 Heat the saucepan up to medium heat and continuously stir the ingredients together until the mixture begins to thicken and turn more translucent. This generally takes between 7 and 9 minutes.

4 Lower the heat once the curd has thickened; continue stirring gently for 1–2 more minutes.

5 Pour into clean, airtight jars. If the jars have been sterilised properly beforehand, the curd will stay safe for up to a month (see page 14 for details). Once the jars have been opened, they should be stored in a refrigerator.

MAKES ABOUT 1 LITRE (2 PINTS)

4 large eggs

280 g (12 oz) caster (or granulated) sugar or light brown sugar

225 g (8 oz) butter, at room temperature

1 tbsp cornflour

Zest and juice from 4 large lemons (when removing zest, avoid getting the bitter white pith in the mix)

TIP
Mixing all ingredients together in one saucepan from the start – even grating your lemons over the pan – will save you clean-up time and trouble.

KIWI LIME MARMALADE

Both kiwis and limes embody the tart snap of summertime flavours and bring to mind seaside holidays sipping citrus drinks and enjoying Key lime pie. Whether this marmalade is given as a present during the summer months when it fits in perfectly with the lightness of al fresco meals or during the winter when it helps to remind the recipient that the sun still exists, there is no question that it will be joyfully received.

MAKES ABOUT 1 LITRE (2 PINTS)

10 ripe kiwis, peeled and chopped roughly

200 g (7 oz) sugar

Pulp, juice and zest from 1 lime

1 Place the chopped kiwis into a saucepan with the sugar and stir gently over a low heat until the sugar has completely dissolved.

2 Add the lime juice, pulp and zest. Bring to the boil and allow to remain bubbling for approximately 10 minutes until the mixture begins to thicken. It is important to continue stirring the mixture so that it does not stick or burn.

3 Pour the marmalade into prepared jars (see page 14 for details). Store in a sterilised jar in a cool, dark cupboard for up to 2 years. Check the seal on the jar before eating anything that has been stored for more than a month; the lid should be firm with no gaps in the seal.

TIP

This already-easy recipe can be made even easier by preparing it using a microwave. Simply combine all ingredients and cook on full power for 5 or 6 minutes. Remove from the microwave and stir through; return to the microwave and cook for 5 to 6 more minutes. Allow to stand at room temperature until it thickens.

STRAWBERRY AND REDCURRANT JAM

Strawberry jam is one of the stalwart foundations of the traditional breakfast table; it is difficult to find anyone who doesn't enjoy the beautiful summertime flavours of the world's favourite berry. By adding the delicious tartness of redcurrants to the already beloved sweetness of strawberry jam, it is possible to marry together the traditional and the exciting. The end result is a flavourful alchemy that will be welcomed at any table.

1. Place all ingredients in a large saucepan and stir through gently to combine. Place over low heat until the sugar has completely dissolved.

2. Increase the heat and allow the mixture to reach boiling point. Keep the mixture on the boil until it reaches the jelly stage (approximately 110°C/220°F on a sugar/jam thermometer). This usually takes 20–25 minutes. Avoid stirring the mixture while it is boiling; instead, use a pastry brush in water to gently brush the jam down the sides of the saucepan.

3. Once the mixture has reached the required temperature, remove from the heat and stir through gently to ensure that no berries have stuck to the bottom of the pan. Spoon into prepared jars (see page 14 for details). Store in a sterilised jar in a cool, dark cupboard for up to 2 years. Check the seal on the jar before eating anything that has been stored for more than a month; the lid should be firm with no gaps in the seal.

MAKES ABOUT 1–1½ LITRES (2–3 PINTS)

750 g (1 lb 10 oz) hulled and coarsely chopped strawberries

750 g (1 lb 10 oz) redcurrants, stalks removed and rinsed

1½ kg (3 lb 5 oz) caster (or granulated) sugar (warmed through, if desired)

Juice of 1 lemon

TIP
Some people swear that warming the sugar makes a huge difference in making jam. To do so, place the sugar in a baking pan in a moderate oven. Warm through for 5 minutes before using.

CHAPTER SIX

Spreads and Chutneys

For those who love savoury treats more than sweet, these preserves will hit the spot every time. From classic chutneys and marmalades to delicious dips, these jars should be a part of every summer picnic. Impress your friends with incredible stand-out flavours.

GREEN TOMATO CHUTNEY

If you have never had a dish made from green tomatoes, you may wonder how an unripened tomato could possibly create something as wonderful as this chutney. Green tomatoes have a delectably sharp tang that is hard to describe and even harder to forget. When you have an abundance of tomatoes that won't ripen before the season ends, don't throw them away! Make this instead.

1 The night before, place the chopped tomatoes and sliced onion in a large bowl. Mix in 4 teaspoons of the salt. Cover with a plate and leave overnight; this makes the tomatoes sweat and reduces the amount of water. (I have left mine for two nights, draining midway through, due to equal parts of being lazy and wanting more sweat to come out.) When you're ready to cook, drain the tomatoes and onions, but do not rinse. Set them aside.

2 Put the vinegar in a large pot and bring to the boil. Add the brown sugar and bring the vinegar back to the boil. Add the sultanas and bring to the boil again.

3 Once you've brought the mixture to the third boil, add the tomatoes and onions and bring the mixture to the boil again. Allow it to continue bubbling while you stir vigorously.

4 Keep the chutney at a brisk simmer/gentle boil for a couple of hours, stirring occasionally as it thickens. Season with salt while cooking.

5 If necessary, when the chutney has turned a golden brown, spoon out a bit of the extra liquid. (This is more necessary if you used fewer tomatoes and have more vinegar than you need. I reserve this to make a sauce.) Just keep letting it simmer until it is thick and soft. When it is ready, you should be able to separate it with your spoon and not have it pour back right away.

6 Spoon into sterilised jars and seal. Unopened, the jars will keep for months in a cool, dark cupboard. Once opened, store in the refrigerator.

TIP
This chutney is begging to go with a rustic bread and a sharp cheddar – it is unbelievably good that way. It's also great as a burger relish.

MAKES ABOUT 1½ LITRES (2½ PINTS)

2–2½ kg (4½ –5½ lb) green tomatoes, roughly chopped

½ –1 onion, finely sliced

10 tsp salt

1 litre (2 pints) cider vinegar

550 g (1¼ lb) packed brown sugar

250 g (9 oz) sultanas, roughly chopped

TIP
This is a great recipe to use up the random bits of hard brown sugar that are hiding in the back of your cupboard.

RED PEPPER CHUTNEY

This chutney makes an absolutely perfect present for anyone on your list who loves rustic, flavourful food. The roasted red peppers become chunky and sweet, just begging to be spread thickly on a farmhouse loaf of bread and served with a sharp cheese. Anyone who loves a more savoury treat will fall in love with this spread.

MAKES ABOUT 550 GRAMS (1 PINT)

3 red peppers

2 spring onions, chopped

2 tbsp olive oil

2–3 cloves garlic, minced

Salt, freshly ground black pepper, and cayenne pepper to taste

1 tbsp cider vinegar

1 Place the red peppers under the grill until the skin begins to scorch, then turn over to roast on the other side. Remove from the oven. If you are removing the skins, place the peppers in a plastic bag. When the peppers have cooled enough to handle, the skins will peel off easily.

2 Remove and discard the pepper stems and seeds. Chop the pulp coarsely, then put into the processor.

3 Meanwhile, in a frying pan, brown the chopped spring onions in the olive oil, then stir in the garlic and seasonings.

4 Add the browned spring onion mixture and the vinegar to the peppers in the food processor. Pulse gently until the desired consistency is achieved.

5 Spoon the chutney into a sterilised pint jar (or two half-pint jars) and seal. Unopened, the jar will keep for months in a cool, dark cupboard. Once opened, store the jar in the refrigerator.

TIP

It is so often recommended that you remove the skins from roasted red peppers that it just about becomes habit, but why not try leaving the skins on for this chutney. The tart scorched elements add a smoky richness.

ROASTED AUBERGINE MARMALADE

The joy of this aubergine marmalade is that it suits so many different purposes that it will make an excellent gift for many different people. While it is a wonderful complement to a simple slice of bread and cheese, it is also a miraculous addition to a curry meal. This is the present guaranteed to impress gourmands who like to make their own richly spiced foods — they will be amazed at how many ways there are to enjoy it.

1 Preheat oven to 200°C (400°F).

2 Place all the ingredients except the chicken broth into a large roasting pan. Stir together to mix well, then put the pan in the oven. Cook for 1–1½ hours until all the liquid has evaporated and the aubergine is browning and beginning to stick to the pan.

3 Scrape the pan, dislodging any spots where the aubergine has begun to stick. Pour in half the broth and cook for 20–30 minutes until the liquid has evaporated.

4 Scrape the pan again and stir in the remaining 120 ml (4 fl oz) broth. Cook for 20 more minutes until the aubergine is fully browned and everything has begun to come together.

5 Pour the mixture into a sterilised pint jar (or two half-pint jars) and seal. Unopened, the jar will keep for months. Once opened, store the jar in the refrigerator.

TIP
The apricots add a counterpoint of sweetness to the marmalade, which makes it complex enough to sit side by side with spicy foods.

MAKES ABOUT 500 GRAMS (1 POUND)

4 medium aubergines, unpeeled, cut into 1-cm (½-in) cubes

3–4 cloves garlic, peeled and minced

3 tbsp grated fresh ginger

100 g (3½ oz) firmly packed brown sugar

1 tsp ground cinnamon

60 ml (2 fl oz) red wine vinegar

1 tbsp oil

1 tbsp soy sauce

40 g (1¼ oz) whole dried apricots, chopped (optional)

240 ml (8 fl oz) chicken broth, divided in two

•••• ••••
103

SAVOURY PUMPKIN SPREAD

For anyone who has fallen in love with pumpkin pies and spiced pumpkin cakes, the creation of a savoury pumpkin spread can be an absolute revelation. This is the present to make for the person who is a little bit quirky; it might be an unexpected taste sensation, but it is one that is sure to be enjoyed.

MAKES ABOUT 900 GRAMS (2 POUNDS)

1 pumpkin

230 g (8 oz) cream cheese

1 tbsp nutritional yeast

½ tsp dried parsley

¼ tsp powdered mustard

¼ tsp garlic powder

Coarse salt and crushed black pepper to taste

TIP
You could use a 425-g (15-oz) tin of pumpkin purée in place of the pumpkin. Simply stir it together with the rest of the ingredients for an easy alternative.

[1] Preheat your oven to 180°C (350°F).

[2] Cut the pumpkin open and remove all the seeds and 'strings'. Save the seeds for roasting – just toss them with a bit of oil and salt and pepper for a delicious snack.

[3] In a greased casserole dish or a pan which has been lined with foil, place the pumpkin skin-side up. You only need to cut the pumpkin into whatever size pieces fit into the pan and oven easily.

[4] Bake in the oven for about an hour or until the pumpkin is very soft to the touch – you should be able to easily slide a fork through the flesh.

[5] Allow the pumpkin to cool until you can work with it. Remove the skin and purée the pumpkin in a food processor until smooth.

[6] Stir together all the ingredients, then adjust the seasonings to taste.

[7] Pour into gift jars. It must be kept refrigerated and eaten within a week. Store in an airtight container in the refrigerator for up to 1 week.

TIP
Depending on what you want this spread to be used for, it can be thinned a bit with a small amount of water.

HOT ARTICHOKE AND SPINACH SPREAD

Years ago I was served a hot artichoke and spinach dip in a restaurant with a perfectly crusty bread. At the first taste, I fell in love and knew that this would made an ideal present for anyone who loves rich flavours with a creamy unctuousness. This recipe makes a wonderful hosting or housewarming present; it works especially well when presented with a loaf of homemade bread.

1 In a mixing bowl, combine all the ingredients. Spoon the mixture into a small greased baking dish.

2 Keep the spread refrigerated until you give it, along with instructions to bake it at 180°C (350°F) for 25–30 minutes, until the top has begun to bubble and brown. It should be baked within a couple of days. Store in an airtight container in the refrigerator for up to 1 week.

MAKES ABOUT 900 GRAMS (2 POUNDS)

230 g (8 oz) cream cheese, softened

60 g (2 oz) sour cream

4 tbsp grated Parmesan cheese

4 tbsp grated Romano cheese

4 tbsp shredded mozzarella cheese

2–3 cloves garlic, peeled and minced

Salt and pepper to taste

400-g (14-oz) tin artichoke hearts, drained and chopped

45 g (1½ oz) thawed and drained frozen chopped spinach

TIP
If you like spinach, add more. This recipe works well with more or less spinach, according to your taste preference.

ROASTED GARLIC AND NUT SPREAD

There are many classic spreads that marry expected flavours; this is not that spread. Roasting the garlic makes it develop a deep sweetness that mellows its flavour, while toasting the nuts grants them a warm saltiness. They are brought together in a creamy, gently sweet mixture. This is a gift for anyone who loves a soft, subtle flavour to accent their meals.

MAKES ABOUT 450 GRAMS (1 POUND)

16 cloves garlic, peeled

4 tbsp olive oil

4 tbsp unblanched sliced almonds, chopped (or other nut)

230 g (8 oz) cream cheese, room temperature

60 g (2 oz) sour cream

2 tsp mustard

1 tsp soy sauce

2 tbsp chopped fresh parsley

1 small onion, chopped

¼ tsp hot sauce (optional)

1 Preheat oven to 140°C (275°F).

2 Drizzle the peeled garlic cloves with the olive oil and place them in a baking pan. Cook for 30 minutes until they begin to become golden. Remove and let cool completely.

3 Meanwhile, in a dry frying pan, toast the nuts until they become lightly golden brown. Allow to cool before continuing.

4 When the nuts and garlic are cool, mix them with the other ingredients in a food processor. Process until the desired consistency is reached.

5 Spoon into jars to present. Keep refrigerated and serve chilled. It should be used within a week.

TIP
Try this recipe with other nuts to see what a difference they can make to both the flavour and the texture. For instance, pecans are wonderful in this recipe.

SUN-DRIED TOMATO AND WALNUT PESTO

If you know someone who loves to cook, then you know someone who will be pleased to be given a jar of this tangy pesto. With the same versatility as traditional pesto, this version is equally happy being used as a spread on bread or crackers, stirred into soups, or mixed through with pasta. But what makes it extra special is the richness of the tomatoes combined with the sweetness of the walnuts; it is perfectly warm and complex.

1 Place all ingredients – except the olive oil – into a food processor and pulse gently.

2 Drizzle the olive oil over the ingredients while processing in order to achieve the desired consistency.

3 Spoon into sterilised jars and seal to present. Store in a sterilised jar in a cool, dark cupboard for up to 1 year. Check the seal on the jar before eating anything that has been stored for more than a month; the lid should be firm with no gaps in the seal.

MAKES ABOUT 350–450 GRAMS (12–16 OZ)

1–2 large garlic cloves, peeled

45 g (1½ oz) fresh basil leaves

45 g (1½ oz) freshly grated Parmesan cheese

45 g (1½ oz) lightly toasted, chopped walnuts

2 tbsp water

60 g (2 oz) chopped marinated sun-dried tomatoes, drained

½ tsp coarse salt

¼ tsp freshly ground black pepper

80 ml (3 fl oz) extra-virgin olive oil

TIP
Try this recipe with different nuts. Milder nuts – like pine nuts, cashews and macadamias – will completely change the way this recipe tastes, making it suitable for a different range of foods.

CHAPTER SEVEN

Oils, Vinegars and Sauces

Every kitchen cupboard will benefit from having a few of these delicious condiments to hand, and who wouldn't love to receive a few as a gift? Elegant, simple to make yet show-stoppingly flavourful – these oils and relishes are sure to delight.

BLACK PEPPER AND CHILLI-INFUSED OIL

Infused oils require only a bit of time and very little effort to make, but they transform into a present that is so impressive and useful that your friends will beg you to make more. Made in a pretty bottle, it becomes a lovely – and delicious! – decoration. Used as a simple dipping sauce with rustic bread, this oil is a spicy, peppery delight. Let your recipient know that it is also fabulous to cook with.

1 Clean and sterilise the bottle or jar you plan to use.

2 Using a kitchen funnel, pour in the oil.

3 Chop the fresh chillies and add them to the oil. Add the additional seasonings.

4 Seal the bottle and let it sit for at least 3 weeks, or present it to the recipient with the request that it be left to sit before being used. Occasionally turning the bottle over during this time period will help to infuse the flavours more evenly. Keep the bottle out of direct sunlight and avoid extreme temperatures. Store in a sterilised bottle or jar in a cool, dark cupboard for up to 3 months.

MAKES ABOUT 700 ML (1¼ PINTS)

600 ml (20 fl oz) virgin olive oil (or rapeseed oil, if preferred)

3–4 fresh hot chillies

2–3 tsp dried chilli flakes

1 tsp peppercorns, any variety (partially crush the peppercorns with a pestle for a spicier oil)

1 bay leaf (optional)

TIP
A simple cold infusion such as this one can be used with any of the hardier spices. Try combining rapeseed oil with nutmeg, whole cloves and a pinch of cayenne pepper for a subtle, warming, autumn oil.

THYME-INFUSED OLIVE OIL

Fresh herbs go together with olive oil like a marriage made in food heaven. While this recipe uses thyme, it is incredibly simple to use any herbs that are the special favourite of your recipient, which allows you to make a stunningly unique and useful present. Delicious just as it is, drizzled over a crusty bit of bread, this oil will also transform any dish that it is cooked in. Give this thyme oil as a gift to a pasta lover and you will be in their good books forever.

MAKES ABOUT 700 ML (1¼ PINTS)

150 g (5½ oz) fresh thyme leaves

2 tsp dried thyme leaves

480 ml (16 fl oz) olive oil (or rapeseed oil, if preferred)

Sprigs of thyme, to garnish

VARIATIONS

Any fresh herb will work, including basil, rosemary, chervil, chives, coriander and mint. Avoid tarragon unless it is very young and fresh, because it can become bitter. Aim for roughly 150 g (5½ oz) of fresh herbs (before they've been blanched) for every 480 ml (16 fl oz) of oil; this can be adjusted to how herby you want your oil.

1 Roughly tear the fresh thyme. Bring a saucepan of water to the boil with a pinch of salt. Blanch the fresh thyme for 5 seconds, then immediately plunge in iced water.

2 Insert the blanched fresh thyme and the dried thyme into a clean, sterilised jar or bottle.

3 Pour in the oil, using a kitchen funnel. Seal the jar. Allow the oil to sit for at least 2 weeks before using it, keeping it out of direct sunlight and avoiding extreme temperature changes. Occasionally turning the bottle over during this time period will help to infuse the flavours more evenly.

4 Present it to your recipient with a delicious rustic bread for dipping. Garnish with sprigs of fresh thyme. Store in a sterilised bottle or jar in a cool, dark cupboard for up to 3 months.

TIP
You can fully infuse an oil and get rid of the 'bits' by running the blanched herbs and oil through a blender and then through muslin cloth. This will give you a gorgeous bright green oil with no pieces of herbs.

KALAMATA OLIVE TAPENADE

If you have ever had a disappointing black olive from a jar, put that experience aside. Kalamata olives are true black olives that are allowed to fully ripen into their dark shades, giving them a rich, delicious flavour that blows all other olives out of the water. For anyone you know who is a bit of an olive connoisseur, this tapenade is a true delight. Present this with a loaf of bread and the jar may be empty before the ribbon is fully removed.

1 In a bowl, mix the olives, garlic, capers, parsley, lemon juice, 1 tablespoon olive oil and anchovy paste (if desired). Season with salt and pepper. Mix well, then refrigerate for 4 hours or overnight to allow the flavours to blend.

2 Pulse the mixture through a food processor until it has the consistency you prefer (the longer you process it, the finer it will be). Add a bit more oil if needed to help get the tapenade to the correct consistency.

3 Spoon into a glass jar for presentation.

4 Present to your recipient with a delicious rustic bread or crackers for dipping. Store in a clean jar in the refrigerator for up to 2 weeks.

MAKES ABOUT 550 GRAMS (1 PINT)

175 g (6 oz) pitted kalamata olives

2–3 cloves garlic, peeled and crushed

1–2 tbsp capers

3 tbsp chopped fresh parsley

1 tbsp lemon juice

1–2 tbsp olive oil (you may need a bit more)

½ tsp anchovy paste (optional)

Freshly cracked black pepper and coarse salt, to taste

TIP
This tapenade works beautifully with other olives, so why not try a blend of your favourites.

BLACKBERRY AND MINT VINEGAR

It is impossible to not fall in love with this vinegar. When I first started exploring flavoured vinegars, I thought it would be difficult to persuade me that sweet and minty flavours could ever work well with the tang of vinegar. I was convinced, however, as soon as this vinegar was drizzled over a salad. Now it is a firm favourite when I am looking to give a present to my food-loving friends.

MAKES ABOUT 480 ML (1 PINT)

225 g (8 oz) fresh mint leaves, washed

375 g (13 oz) blackberries, washed (raspberries can also be used)

480 ml (16 fl oz) white vinegar

1. Place the mint leaves in a sterilised glass jar and bruise them with a pestle or wooden spoon. Spoon in the berries, crushing them on top of the mint.

2. Pour in the vinegar, cover the jar with a lid and allow the mixture to steep. If using fresh, it can be used after it has set overnight. Simply pour over a salad or other dish, enjoying the infused berries and mints.

3. If you want to keep the vinegar for longer or you do not want any solids, allow the vinegar to sit for about a week (up to 2 weeks, but note that it gets stronger the longer it sits). Remove the lid and strain the vinegar through a fine sieve into a clean glass container for presentation. Vinegars keep for just about forever. If you leave the berries in rather than strain them out, you may find that the vinegar begins to appear cloudy.

TIP
This style of vinegar can be easily adapted to other combinations – just mix a soft fruit and a fresh herb for a beautiful flavour. Consider strawberries and basil or peach and mint for a light summery feel.

POMEGRANATE AND CORIANDER RELISH

This relish is the perfect gift for someone who loves to get adventurous in the kitchen. Prepare to be amazed and impressed by the burst of flavours that this relish gives to meat dishes — especially pork or any meat that goes well with a cranberry sauce, such as turkey. It can be used cold as a marinade for the meat or warmed through to serve with the meat; either way, it is absolutely delicious.

1. Remove the seeds and juice from the pomegranates and set aside.

2. Gently heat the olive oil in a saucepan over medium heat. Cook the chopped onion through until it just begins to turn golden brown. Add the pomegranate seeds and juice, the lemon juice, molasses, salt and pepper. Cook for a few minutes until the juices begin to reduce slightly and begin to thicken. Remove from heat.

3. Stir the coriander through the pomegranate mixture. Let the relish cool.

4. Place the relish in a jar to present as a gift. Store this relish in the refrigerator for up to 1 week.

MAKES ABOUT 550 GRAMS (1 PINT)

2 pomegranates

2 tbsp olive oil

½ small onion, chopped

1 tbsp lemon juice

1 tbsp pomegranate molasses

Salt and pepper to taste

90 g (3 oz) chopped fresh coriander

TIP
Try using fresh mint instead of the coriander for a relish that is quite zesty on lamb.

DEVIL'S MEAT SAUCE

There is an art to making a hot sauce that packs a punch but keeps you coming back for more. The secret is to combine the flavours in such a way that they take on a mellow and sweet base, which lulls your tongue into a false sense of security before the chillies come out to play. This Devil's Meat Sauce is the present to give to the person on your list who is convinced that food isn't delicious until they can feel the burn.

MAKES ABOUT 115 GRAMS (4 OZ)

3 tbsp Strawberry and Redcurrant Jam (page 96), or another jam

1 tbsp brown sugar

2 tbsp lemon juice

1–2 tbsp hot chilli sauce

2 tbsp tomato paste

Salt and pepper to taste

1 Put all the ingredients into a saucepan and warm through over medium heat just until the mixture boils and the sugar melts, stirring constantly.

2 Remove from the heat and allow to cool before pouring into a presentation glass jar. Store in a clean jar in the refrigerator for up to 2 months.

TIP
This meat sauce is perfect as a hot dipping sauce, but also try it as a marinade. The blend of hot and sweet is excellent with meat, especially venison.

HOT AND SWEET COLA BBQ SAUCE

While there is a great equality between the sexes when it comes to the kitchen, barbecue sauce seems to be one of those gift items that really impresses the men. This sauce is a particularly pleasing combination, as it blends together a sweetness and a heat, which makes it ideal for using straight onto food or as a marinade for preparing meats that are about to hit the barbecue. However it is used, it is guaranteed to please.

1 Mix together all the ingredients except the lemon juice in a saucepan over medium heat. Bring to the boil, then reduce the heat to a simmer. Allow the mixture to simmer until it thickens, about 30–45 minutes.

2 Remove the mixture from the heat and stir in the lemon juice. Adjust the final seasonings to taste.

3 Decant the sauce, while it is still hot, into sterilised jars. Seal, and present as a gift. Can be stored in the refrigerator for up to 2 months.

TIP
Try making this with Dr Pepper or root beer for an interesting twist.

MAKES ABOUT 1 LITRE (2¼ PINTS)

600 ml (20 fl oz) cola (the brand does not matter, but it should NOT be diet)

3–4 cloves garlic, peeled and crushed into a paste

½ tsp coarse salt

340 g (12 oz) ketchup

60 ml (2 fl oz) cider or malt vinegar

2 tbsp soy sauce (optional)

1 tbsp chilli powder

1–2 tsp hot chilli sauce, or to taste

Coarsely ground black pepper to taste

2 tbsp lemon juice

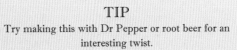

CHAPTER EIGHT

Savoury Treats

If you've ever hated to take the same old boring bottle of wine or box of chocolates as a hostess gift, this chapter featuring savoury snacks is the answer to your prayers. Anyone who shows up bearing one of these delicious treats will be a welcome guest.

GARLIC AND BROWN SUGAR CHEESE BALL

It seems like an odd flavour combination, but this is such a crowd pleaser that it is always best to bring two. The sweetness of the brown sugar is a perfect complement to the garlic and spiced cheese – no one is quite sure why that works, but it truly does. This makes a wonderful hostess present – especially when presented with buttery crackers – and an ideal gift for that overworked host who likes a non-traditional treat.

1 Mix together the garlic, cream cheese, cheddar cheese, salt and pepper. Shape gently into two balls around the size of a tennis ball, and chill in the refrigerator for at least 1 hour.

2 Meanwhile, heat together the butter and brown sugar until the sugar is incorporated with the butter – you can do this either on the hob or in the microwave, but be sure to stir continually so that they do not separate. Allow to cool to room temperature.

3 Spread the brown sugar mix over the chilled cheese balls. This process does involve a fair bit of scooping up the mixture and letting it drip back down; you want to have a good coverage of the brown sugar mix over the entire ball.

4 Sprinkle the crushed nuts over the ball or roll the ball in the crushed nuts if you don't mind getting your hands a little messy.

5 Chill before presenting as a gift; serve at room temperature with crackers. Store covered in the refrigerator for up to 1 week.

TIP
This recipe can easily be varied with other cheeses and nut combinations. One of my favourites is to add a teaspoon of smoked paprika to the cheese mix and then to roll the ball in almond flakes.

MAKES 2 BALLS

1–2 cloves garlic, minced

230 g (8 oz) cream cheese, softened

175 g (6 oz) grated sharp cheddar cheese

Salt and pepper to taste

60 g (2 oz) butter, softened

50 g (1¾ oz) brown sugar

4 tbsp chopped pecans

OLD-FASHIONED SOFT PRETZELS

Everyone who has ever tried a soft-baked pretzel knows that there is something particularly delicious about a pretzel that goes far beyond what a bready-food should be. While they give the impression of being a complicated, difficult treat to make, pretzels are really quite achievable, even for beginners.

MAKES 12 LARGE PRETZELS

7-g (¼-oz) packet active dry yeast

2 tbsp brown sugar

1⅛ tsp salt

350 ml (12 fl oz) warm water

340 g (12 oz) plain flour

115 g (4 oz) bread flour

1 litre (1¾ pints) water

4 tbsp baking soda

2 tbsp sugar, mixed with 1 tsp ground cinnamon (or 2 tbsp melted butter mixed with 2 tbsp coarse kosher salt)

TIP

These freeze well. You can make these in advance and defrost before giving them.

1. Mix together the yeast, brown sugar and salt in 350 ml (12 fl oz) warm water. Set aside to dissolve.

2. Sieve together the two flours into a large bowl. Pour in the yeast liquid, mixing well. Work the dough with your hands until it is smooth and pliable.

3. Place the dough in a large greased bowl (turning the dough once so that the grease is also on the top of the dough). Set it in a warm place for 1 hour to rise.

4. Once the dough has risen, cut it into 12 equal pieces. Working on a floured surface, roll out each piece into a long, thin roll (the rolls should be as thin as pencils, as they will rise again before being baked). If the dough is difficult to work with, roll out each portion halfway and let it rest before rolling it the rest of the way. Turn each rolled tube of dough into a pretzel shape.

5. In a saucepan, bring the litre (1¾ pints) of water and the baking soda to the boil. One by one, put the formed pretzels in the boiling water. Leave them in the water until they rise to the surface and float. When they do, remove and set aside on a sheet pan.

6. After the boil bath, allow the pretzels to rise for 15–20 minutes. Preheat the oven to 230°C (450°F) while they are rising.

7. Bake for 8–10 minutes or until the pretzels turn a deep golden brown.

8. Remove them from the oven and immediately brush with a mixture of sugar and sprinkle with cinnamon (or 2 tablespoons melted butter and coarse salt for a savoury pretzel). Let cool, wrap loosely in parchment paper and present in a gift box. Store in an airtight container in a dark cupboard for up to a week.

TIP

Do not be tempted to rush the rising time. If you don't allow your dough to rise fully, it will be a misery to work with when you try to shape it into pretzels.

TWO-WEEK BREAD AND BUTTER PICKLES

This traditional favourite is also an incredibly easy present to make. Planning ahead means that you can give this as a gift that can be opened right away, but if you need a quick present, just tell your recipient to let the anticipation build for two weeks. These pickles make a delicious snack on their own, but they are also great sliced on sandwiches or tossed into salads.

1 Sterilise jars in advance.

2 The night before cooking, or at least 4 hours in advance, prepare the cucumbers. If they are baby cucumbers, they may be left whole. If they are larger, slice into rounds, as you wish. Place prepared cucumbers with the sliced onions in a large bowl. Mix in the pickling salt. Cover with a cloth and allow to sweat.

3 Drain off the brine and rinse the cucumbers and onions.

4 In a large kettle, mix together the vinegars, the sugar and all the seasonings. Bring to the boil.

5 As soon as the vinegar mixture boils, add the cucumbers and onions. Bring again to the boil. Remove from the heat. Using a slotted spoon, immediately fill the prepared jars to 4–5 cm (1½–2 in) from the rim. Spoon in 2 cm (1 in) of the hot vinegar on top of the pickles.

6 Seal the jars and set aside for 2 weeks. Store in a sterilised jar in a cool, dark cupboard. Once open, store for up to 3 months in the refrigerator.

MAKES ABOUT 3 LITRES (5 PINTS)

1 kg (2½ lb) pickling cucumbers (the fresher the better)

450 g (1 lb) white onions, thinly sliced

250 g (9 oz) pickling or kosher salt

300 ml (10 fl oz) white vinegar (5% acidity)

240 ml (8 fl oz) malt vinegar (5% acidity)

450 g (1 lb) sugar

1 tbsp mustard seeds

1 tsp dried chilli flakes

1 tsp allspice berries

Pinch ground allspice

1 tsp whole cloves

Pinch ground cloves

½ tsp powdered turmeric

1 tsp whole peppercorns

TIP
For a spicy present, try replacing the cucumbers with jalapeños. Just be careful to remove the seeds first (and wear gloves when working with them!). They will be sweeter than normal jalapeños, yet with a spicy kick that make them fabulous in sandwiches.

PICKLED EGGS WITH BEETROOT

I was all grown up before I ever realised that not all pickled eggs are a deep, beautiful magenta. My grandmother never made a pickled egg that wasn't made side by side with beetroot and now I can't think why anyone would want a boring old white one. This is a present that equally suits the country traditionalist who loves a pickled egg and someone who will find a bit of fun in eating a purple food that didn't start out in life that colour.

MAKES ABOUT 1 LITRE (1 QUART)

425-g (15-oz) tin beetroot, sliced or whole (I prefer to use baby beetroot)

12 hard-boiled eggs

120 ml (4 fl oz) cider or white vinegar

120 ml (4 fl oz) water

100 g (3½ oz) sugar

½ tsp ground allspice

½ tsp ground nutmeg

½ tsp ground cinnamon

¼ tsp whole cloves

1. Drain the beetroot, reserving the juice.

2. Place the eggs and beetroot in a sterilised litre jar and set aside.

3. In a saucepan, mix together the vinegar, water, sugar, beet juice and spices. Bring to the boil and allow the sugar to completely dissolve. Boil at a high heat for 10 minutes.

4. Remove the mixture from the heat and pour it over the eggs and beetroot. Seal the jar and set it aside to cool.

5. For the next few hours, flip the jar over several times to ensure that the pickling liquid is coating all of the eggs evenly (otherwise, you'll end up with strange splotches).

6. Present in a sealed jar. Store in a sterilised jar (avoiding extremes in humidity). Once they are open, store for up to 3 months in the refrigerator.

TIP
These are great (and look wonderful) sliced in a green salad.

MIXED VEGETABLE PICKLES

Mixed vegetable pickles deserve to be far more popular. They are tangy and delicious, with the added benefit of being more than a little good for you. For everyone who has ever been disappointed to get a jar that has too many carrots and not enough cauliflower (or vice versa), making a homemade batch makes perfect sense. This is a great present for the snackers on your list who like a bit of sour.

1 Sterilise 2 litre (quart) jars. Place equal amounts of garlic and chilli flakes or chopped chillies in the bottom of each jar.

2 Combine all the vegetables in a large bowl. Then pack the jars tightly with a mix of the vegetables.

3 Mix the brine ingredients in a saucepan. Over high heat, bring the solution strongly to the boil. Immediately pour the solution into the prepared vegetable jars to within 1 or 2 cm (½ or 1 in) from the rim.

4 Add ¼ teaspoon of vegetable oil to the top of each jar and seal.

5 Give the sealed jars of pickled vegetables as presents. Tell your recipients to let them sit for 2 or more weeks before opening, for best results. (I like to mark the 'ready' date on top of the jar.) Store in a sterilised jar (avoiding extremes in humidity). Once they are open, store for up to 3 months in the refrigerator.

TIP
This recipe can easily be changed to accommodate your favourite vegetables; try using carrots and jalapeños.

MAKES ABOUT 2 LITRES (2 QUARTS)

3–6 cloves garlic, peeled

2–4 tsp dried chilli flakes or 2 fresh chillies, chopped

1 cauliflower head, broken into small florets

1 broccoli head, broken into small florets

1 green pepper, cut into 2-cm (1-in) pieces

1 red pepper, cut into 2-cm (1-in) pieces

125 g (4½ oz) small onions, peeled

1 large cucumber, sliced into rounds

½ tsp vegetable oil

BRINE
1½ litres (2½ pints) water

700 ml (1¼ pints) white vinegar

100 g (3½ oz) pickling or kosher salt

•••• ••••

135

SUN-DRIED COURGETTE

Drying courgette is one of the absolute best ways to deal with a bumper crop. Even if you don't have a garden full of vegetables, it would be worth buying some courgette just to dry. These make a perfect present because they last just about forever, and they make an incredible addition to soups and pastas through the cold winter when summer vegetables seem long gone. A perfect gift for anyone who loves to cook.

MAKES ABOUT 225 GRAMS (8 OZ)

2–3 large courgettes, thinly sliced on the diagonal

3 tbsp coarse salt

Seasonings as preferred (I like to use a mix of dried oregano, basil and garlic)

1 Toss the sliced courgette with the salt and set aside for up to 24 hours. Drain off liquids every few hours, or more frequently if desired. Adding a weight to the top of the courgette will help press the liquid out faster. Do not rinse.

2 After your final draining, toss the courgette slices with your seasonings, then arrange them on a greased flat baking sheet. Place in a low oven (120°C/250°F) for 2 hours or until they have greatly reduced in size, yet are still soft.

3 Remove the slices from the oven, let cool and place in a jar to present. Store in a clean, airtight container in a cool, dark cupboard (too much light can discolour the courgette) for up to 1 year. These can be frozen if desired by your recipient.

TIP

These can also be dried in a food dehydrator, or if it's a warm summer, they can be strung on a string and dried in the heat outside.

BANANA PEPPERS STUFFED WITH FETA AND PROSCIUTTO AND MARINATED IN OIL

This is one of those food items that you pay premium for at a speciality food shop, yet is surprisingly easy to make at home. Anyone who loves the salty blend of prosciutto and feta will fall in love with these fantastic little peppers. They are delicious on their own, but they can also take part in a wonderful tapas spread. These are a real treat for those on your list who love really decadent, flavourful food.

1 Drain the peppers, reserving the oil if they were marinated or discarding the vinegar if they were pickled.

2 Slice fine fingers of feta cheese and wrap each one in a single sheet of prosciutto ham.

3 Gently insert the rolled cheese into the pepper, using your finger to press it firmly to the bottom of the pepper.

4 Pack the peppers in a sterilised jar, cover with the reserved oil or sesame oil, and seal. Once opened, keep in the refrigerator for up to 2 weeks.

MAKES ONE 240 ML (HALF-PINT) JAR

1 jar pickled banana peppers in vinegar or marinated banana peppers in oil (about 1 dozen peppers)

About 230 g (½ lb) feta cheese

8–12 sheets prosciutto ham

Sesame oil to cover (if peppers were in vinegar)

TIP
There are several different types of peppers that are preserved in oil; each has a different flavour that would suit adaptations from this basic recipe. A sweet piquante pepper, for example, is wonderful with cream cheese wrapped in prosciutto.

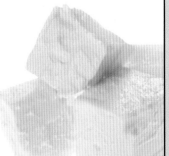

Index

Credits

Unless specified below, all images are the copyright of Quintet Publishing Ltd, and may not be reproduced without prior written permission. While every effort has been made to credit contributors, Quintet Publishing would like to apologise should there have been any omissions or errors – and would be pleased to make the appropriate correction for future editions of the book.

T = TOP, B = BELOW, C = CENTRE, L = LEFT,
R = RIGHT

DIVERTIMENTI www.divertimenti.co.uk: 8T-R.

ISTOCK: 62T; 121T; 113T.

LAKELAND: 8T-L Thermometer, ref. 8776, £7.49; 8B-L Preserving Bars, ref. 13176, £4.99; Buttons, ref. 13174, £4.99; 9B-L Bakingenious Non-stick Baking Sheet, ref. 12371, £12.99. Order online: www.lakeland.co.uk. Order by phone: 015394 88100 50.

SHUTTERSTOCK: 8T-C; 8B-L; 9T-L; 9T-C; 9T-R; 9B-C; 9B-R; 13R; 29T, B; 30T, B; 33T, B; 34T, B; 37T, B; 38T, B; 41T, B; 43T; 44T, B; 47T, B; 48T, B; 51T, B; 52T, B; 55T, B; 57T, B; 58T, B; 61T, B; 62B; 65T, B; 66T, B; 69T; 71T, B; 72T, B; 75T, B; 76T, B; 79T, B; 80T, B; 83T, B; 85T, B; 86T, B; 89T, B; 90T, B; 93T, B; 94T, B; 97T, B; 99T, B; 100T, B; 103T, B; 104T, B; 107T, B; 108T, B; 111T, B; 113B; 114B; 117B; 118T, B; 121B; 122B; 125T, B; 127T, B; 128T, B; 131T, B; 132T, B; 135T, B; 136T, B; 139T, B.

STOCKFOOD: 10 © Finley, Marc O. / StockFood; 12 © Errico, Jerry / StockFood.

AUTHOR'S ACKNOWLEDGEMENTS

This is the first book I have ever put together and without the help of those around me, it might well have gone to press as little more than a stack of recipes scribbled on scraps of paper. My gratitude goes out to the entire **Quintet Publishing** team who helped me every step of the way, but most especially to **Carly Beckerman-Boys** who found me and guided me through the process of creating my book outline; **Martha Burley**, my gracious project editor who kept nudging me gently in the right direction and made sure I made it through the process completely unscathed; **Zoë White**, who took care of all the important details – not least of which was taking care of my beloved jars – and **Anya Hayes** who took me masterfully through the murky middle period of the project in Martha's stead. An additional debt of gratitude has to be paid to **Cary Hull**, the brave copyeditor who took on the task of making sure my directions made sense and juggled all of the conversions between imperial, metric and my own casually styled measurements.

Finally, my full appreciation and love goes to all of those who bravely tasted my recipes during the trial periods and resolutely embraced the heavy caloric workload. **Rolle Nieminen** remains the best friend a girl could have and has the iron stomach that all cooks admire; **Dr Chuw Golledge** kept me stocked up in all the support and love I could have needed, as well as provided the best apricots; and my brother, **Chris McCloskey**, who has always kept the home fires burning.